Campaigning

The A to Z of Public Advocacy

HAWKSMERE

Campaigning

The A to Z of Public Advocacy

by DES WILSON

with Leighton Andrews

Viva Books Private Limited

New Delhi • Mumbai • Chennai • Kolkata • Hyderabad • Bangalore

First Indian Edition 2006

VIVA BOOKS PRIVATE LIMITED

- 4747/23, Ansari Road, Daryaganj, New Delhi 110 002
  E-mail: vivadelhi@vivagroupindia.net, Tel. 23258325, 23283121
- 215-216 New Apollo Estate, Mogra Lane, Andheri (E), Mumbai 400 069
  E-mail: vivamumbai@vivagroupindia.net, Tel. 56997844, 56997845
- Jamals Fazal Chambers, 26 Greams Road, Chennai 600 006
  E-mail: vivachennai@vivagroupindia.net, Tel. 28290304, 28294241
- B-103, Jindal Towers, 21/1A/3 Darga Road, Kolkata 700 017
  E-mail: vivakolkata@vivagroupindia.net, Tel. 22836381, 22816713
- 7, Sovereign Park Apartments, 56-58, K. R. Road, Basavanagudi, Bangalore 560 004
  E-mail: vivabangalore@vivagroupindia.net, Tel.26607409, 26607410
- 101-102 Mughal Marc Apartments, Narayanguda, Hyderabad 500 029
  E-mail: vivahyderabad@vivagroupindia.net, Tel. 27564481, 27564482

Published by arrangement with

Thorogood Publishers Limited
10-12 Rivington Street
London EC2A 3DU,
UK

ISBN 81-309-0256-7

Published by Vinod Vasishtha for Viva Books Private Limited, 4262/3 Ansari Road, Daryaganj, New Delhi 110 002. Printed by Sanat Printers, Kundli - 131028.

To

Eamonn Casey

whose brave and tireless campaigning for the homeless and for Shelter will always be an inspiration.

LEIGHTON ANDREWS

Leighton Andrews is head of public affairs at the BBC. Immediately prior to joining the BBC he was joint managing director of the Saatchi and Saatchi-owned PR consultancy, the Rowland Company, and before that managing director of the lobbying company Sallingbury Casey. His previous lobbying experience was gained as director of the UN International Year of Shelter for the Homeless, as parliamentary officer for Age Concern England and as parliamentary assistant to the All Party Group for Pensioners. Many of the lobbying campaigns in which he has been involved have been covered in the national press and the broadcast media. He has frequently advised non-profit organisations on their lobbying on a *pro bono* basis, and has acted as honorary parliamentary adviser to a number of campaigning organisations, including the Friends of John McCarthy.

DES WILSON

Des Wilson is Britain's best-known campaigner, with a track record equal to that of anyone in the world. Previously a journalist (he has been a columnist on the *Guardian* and *The Observer*), he began his campaigning career as the first director of Shelter, the National Campaign for the Homeless, and built it into one of the country's most effective campaigning charities. In the 1980s he became a major figure in the environmental movement. He led the campaign that won lead-free petrol for the whole of Europe, became chairman of Friends of the Earth and campaign director for FoE International, and was chosen by ITN as environmentalist of the decade. He has been chairman of Citizen Action, of the Campaign for Freedom of Information and of Parents against Tobacco. In 1982 he directed the Liberal Democrats' general election campaign and for it won *PR Week*'s award for an outstanding individual contribution to the communications industry.

Des Wilson is now UK director of public affairs with Burson-Marsteller, the world's largest public relations consultancy, and in that capacity led the acclaimed campaign which in 1993 saved the Crossrail project. He is a well-known journalist, writer and broadcaster, and is the author of 11 books, including a novel on campaigning called *Campaign*. Two of those books, *Pressure* and *Citizen Action*, were on campaigning; they are now both out of print and this latest book draws on their contents, updating and enlarging upon them.

Contents

Introduction

Nearly ten years back, in 1984, I wrote a book called *Pressure: The A to Z of Campaigning in Britain*. Later, in 1986, this was followed by *Citizen Action: Taking Action in Your Community*. The first of these was about national campaigning; the second was about campaigning at local level. Both are now out of print.

This third book is an updated version of them both, drawing extensively on their contents but adding fresh experiences and insights gained in the intervening decade.

Some introductory points may be helpful.

First, about the case histories and illustrations.

To illustrate the chapter on local campaigning and the Leighton Andrews chapter on lobbying, we've devised a small number of fictitious campaigns, based on the non-existent town of Smithsville. These are described at the beginning of Chapter 3.

For the purposes of the sections on national campaigning I've drawn on those campaigns I've been personally associated with, including Shelter, the Campaign for Lead-Free Air (CLEAR), Friends of the Earth (FoE), the Campaign for Freedom of Information (FoI), Parents against Tobacco (PaT), the 1992 Liberal Democrat general election campaign, and the Crossrail second reading campaign.

I was director of Shelter from when it was launched in 1966 to 1971. Shelter was created to raise money to help the homeless and to campaign for more enlightened housing policies. It was one of the first major charities to challenge the limits of charity law by also campaigning as a non-party political pressure group. In the late 1960s it raised millions of pounds, contributed to radical changes in the treatment of the homeless, helped to pioneer housing aid and advice centres and affected housing policy in a variety of constructive ways. It still exists today, confronting, alas, a fresh housing crisis caused by the appalling housing policies of the Thatcher years.

Throughout its brief existence, I was chairman of CLEAR. CLEAR was launched in January 1982: by April 1983 it had achieved its single objective – the decision to phase lead out of petrol. It then campaigned for the introduction of lead-free petrol across the whole of the European Community, and it later worked constructively with the petrol companies to encourage motorists to use the product – a classic case of former opponents subsequently uniting on common ground.

From 1983 to 1987 I was chairman of FoE. If CLEAR was a single-issue pressure group, FoE was (and still is) an 'issues in context' campaign. In other words, it campaigns single-mindedly on particular issues such as the protection of Sites of Special Scientific Interest in Britain or tropical rain forests in Third World countries, but always within an overall context, in this case the environmental cause.

For six years I was chairman of FoI. It was launched in 1984 and in ten years has produced more private members' legislation than almost any other organisation in history, thanks mainly to the determination and skill of its director, Maurice Frankel. Its bills have covered access to personal records, health and safety and environmental information, and access to town hall meetings and papers, so that while it has yet to achieve its ideal of an FoI Act, it has achieved nearly half of what a full FoI Act would allow.

In 1990–91 I was chairman of PaT. Another single-issue campaign, its objective was to reduce the sale of cigarettes to children under 16. Launched in 1990, it quickly achieved its aim of tougher laws and heavier fines to control what were already illegal sales. Under its effective director Jane Dunmore it now campaigns to ensure that the law is properly enforced.

The Crossrail second reading campaign is an exception to the above in that it was extremely short term, lasting barely over a month, and backed by a coalition of London business and citizen organisations. Its aim was to force a second reading for the Crossrail bill and in this it succeeded. My involvement was in my capacity as director of public affairs with the consultancy Burson-Marsteller.

The Liberal Democrat 1992 general election campaign began for me, its unpaid director, two years earlier when the party was in single figures in the polls. The aim was not to win the election – that was clearly an impossibility – but to achieve a respectable result, a launching pad for growth later in the decade. Our private target was 20/20 – 20 per cent of the popular vote and 20 MPs. In fact we won 18 per cent of the vote but did return a parliamentary group of 20.

These, then, are the national campaigns, spanning 26 years, which I will refer to throughout this book.

A word, now, about Part Two. This is divided into chapters on national and local campaigning. However, many of the ideas and suggestions are applicable to both types. No problem is the same; no campaign is the same. To get the best from my experience you have, as you read, to be constantly applying it to your own circumstances.

I should address one question here: Whom is this book for? Primarily it is for the concerned citizen ... for the individual fighting for his or her own rights or freedoms, for the group seeking to put an issue on the political agenda or to combat deprivation or injustice. But it is also for the local community seeking to achieve less dramatic objectives – maybe to get better street-lighting, or to persuade the local council to create better recreational facilities for its children. It is also for companies or other institutions, and their public affairs advisers, who have legitimate interests to defend and every right to defend them. For, as I argue in Chapter 1, everyone – whether perceived as rich or poor, powerful or weak – is entitled to make his or her case in the court of public opinion. I may have campaigned single-mindedly over the years but I have never expected or sought a one-sided contest, just an even playing field.

Finally, I've tried to be practical and to the point. The book is, therefore, inevitably fragmented. Really, it is a scrapbook ... a scrapbook of anecdotes and experiences, ideas and suggestions.

I've always rather enjoyed dipping into other people's scrapbooks. I hope you do also.

Des Wilson

November 1993

Abbreviations

The following abbreviated titles for campaigns are generally used throughout this book:

CLEAR	Campaign for Lead-Free Air
FoE	Friends of the Earth
FoI	Campaign for Freedom of Information
PaT	Parents against Tobacco

Part One

The Principles

1 Advocate in the Court of Public Opinion

... the role and rights of the campaigner

... the principles of campaigning

We're all entitled to our day in court. Rich or poor, powerful or weak, we're entitled to speak for ourselves ... to fight our corner. Or to be properly represented – to have an advocate who knows how to work the system and how to present our case.

As it is in a court of law, so it should be in the 'court of public opinion' or in the 'courts' where public policy is determined – in Whitehall and Westminster, or in our local town hall. Wherever people are in a position to judge us or make decisions that affect us, we should have the right to be heard or be represented.

That's why I've always described myself as 'an advocate in the court of public opinion'.

In my time I've been an advocate for the homeless and their rights to be treated compassionately; an advocate for our rights to breathe clean air, drink clean water and generally be protected from pollution; an advocate for our rights to information ... and for much more. I've been a public affairs adviser, an advocate for the rights of shopkeepers to trade when they wish, and an advocate for one form of public expenditure in preference to another.

That's what pressure groups and lobbyists are. They're advocates.

There are other parallels too ...

As in a court of law, it's essential that in the court of public opinion both sides of the case are argued and heard. No one condemns a lawyer because he or she is a prosecutor rather than a defence counsel. We accept that both are needed. So it should be in our wider court.

And just as no one condemns barristers for arguing their case with passion, for fighting with single-minded determination to present the strongest case for their client and to undermine their opponents, so no one should condemn the advocates in our wider court for doing the same.

Public advocacy is not just a right; it's a necessity. It ensures balanced debate – that decision-makers are more likely to hear all the facts, better able to judge the level of opposition or support and, as a result, hopefully more likely to make better-informed, fairer and more popular decisions.

Public advocacy underwrites the health of our democracy. It ensures that there's more to it than the occasional vote; that there's participation between elections; that those in power find it difficult to exceed the authority they've been given; that minority views are voiced; that there is proper surveillance of the governmental machine by people who are specialists in every area; that each pressure group or vested interest has to test its case in competition with another; and that individuals and groups are given the confidence and the weapons to fight on their own behalf.

There are, of course, politicians and others within the governmental process who resent the proliferation of public advocates. To them the pressure group in particular is a damned nuisance. It makes it more difficult to impose decisions; more difficult to govern. For my part, I don't care that the country is more difficult to govern; I think it *should* be difficult to govern if the alternative is easy-going or ill-informed acquiescence with the exercise of centralised power. Countries that are easy to govern are countries that are easy to misgovern. Countries with dictatorships are easy to govern; democracies are more difficult.

The fact is that national and local authorities have enormous power over our lives. So do other big institutions, from multi-national companies to privatised industries and even to our increasingly independent health and education services. Their power is increased by technologies that encourage centralised control. We cannot rely on elected councillors or Members of Parliament to protect our freedoms and interests; quite apart from the fact that they get drawn into the system until the majority of them are part of it, it is a physical impossibility for them to know all that is happening and to represent us on every issue.

We have had to learn to become our own advocates. We have found that by grouping together into organisations we can develop expertise on our subject and the power to draw attention to it or campaign about it.

A whole 'industry' has developed – in two parts. On one hand, there are citizen pressure groups, thousands and thousands of them, from big nationally known ones with 50,000 or more members or supporters to little local ones.

On the other hand, more and more professionals in the public relations industry are now known as public affairs or governmental affairs advisers and assist companies and institutions to make their case on public policy issues. It is surprising how often there is common ground between the two kinds of advocate, for often the opponent is the system itself.

I have worked as an advocate on both sides of this 'industry' – I have been a prosecutor and a defender. But, wherever possible, I've tried to be a unifier, encouraging the two sides to identify the real problem and to tackle it together.

Over the years I have developed a philosophy about public advocacy. It begins with a passionate belief in its importance for our democracy and from there it extends to a conviction that just as there are rules of behaviour that apply in courts of law, so there are principles that should apply to campaigning in the court of public opinion.

When it comes to public advocacy, almost every case is argued on the grounds that it is in 'the public interest'. Thus, anti-smoking groups argue that smoking is the major cause of preventable ill-health while tobacco companies point to the employment they create and the income that tobacco tax brings to the national exchequer. If the battle ground is the 'public interest', then the battle should be fought under rules or on the basis of principles that serve the public interest. One key principle is that the campaigner has a responsibility to his or her cause to campaign well.

Below I list ten principles that I have tried to apply to my campaigns.

1 *Tell the Truth*

How can the public interest be served by decisions taken on the basis of inaccurate so-called facts, untrue claims, deliberate misinformation or 'loaded' research?

In a court of law, witnesses for both sides swear to tell the truth, the whole truth and nothing but the truth. Of course, it would be unrealistic to claim that they always do. But at least it is the advocate's role to encourage it and to tease it out from the other side. The whole aim of the exercise is to establish the truth – guilt or innocence, liability or non-liability. So it should be in the court of public opinion. We either believe in our case or we don't. If we do, we should fight it on the basis of the facts. If we don't, we should ask ourselves what we're doing and why, and how it is serving the public interest.

2 IF YOU DON'T LIKE HARD WORK, DON'T GET INVOLVED

If this is not going to be a high priority in your life, forget it. Campaigning is hard work. Without dedication, effort and persistence, you'll fail. If you're not prepared to sacrifice yourself, you won't persuade others to.

Just as a casino nearly always wins because it has the resources to ride out its bad run and the gambler invariably doesn't have the resources, so 'the system' depends on having more stamina than you – more resources, more time and unlimited capacity for delay. One of the first responses to your campaign will be to test your persistence.

The cause can't afford your failure. Every failure makes a fresh initiative on the same issue more difficult. Thus anyone who adopts a cause and undertakes a campaign has a responsibility to do it properly – to work hard and to dedicate himself or herself to its success.

3 MAINTAIN A SENSE OF PERSPECTIVE

Everybody who runs a campaign tends to believe that his or her cause is most vital and urgent. For instance, some anti-lead campaigners believe lead pollution to be the biggest threat to mankind short of nuclear war. Some have actually said this. My own view is that lead pollution is one of a number of serious environmental health hazards that should be eliminated. This should be done as soon as is practicable. It is a hazard to health and that is all that need be said. There is no need to exaggerate the issue.

The effective campaigner at all costs avoids becoming a fanatic. The dangers are manifold: first, a complete inability to see the wood for the trees, so that every action he or she takes is given equal weight; second, a tendency to paranoia, so that anyone who is even sceptical – let alone arguing the opposite side – is automatically assumed to have sinister motives and often is criticised or condemned with no evidence whatsoever in a way that discredits the campaigners; third, misapplication of persistence to the point where they are written off as cranks, so that although the campaigners may be completely right in their diagnosis of the problem or in their proposed reforms they undermine the cause. Finally, perspective is necessary to preserve your own sanity. To be excessively committed is to risk obsession – it is a fine balance – and this in turn can result in a distorted personality.

To sum up, the object should be to make the strongest possible case for the earliest possible action consistent with not raising serious doubts in the minds of others as to whether your judgement can be trusted. A sense of perspective enhances credibility; lack of perspective will leave you talking to yourself.

4 ABHOR VIOLENCE

It should be an underlying principle of any campaign within a democracy that it is pursued without resort to violence.

As an Australian campaigner once wrote:

> Violence as a means for obtaining social change has several severe flaws: it often causes suffering; it abdicates moral superiority and alienates potential support; it requires secrecy and hence leads to undemocratic decision-making; and, if successful, it tends to lead towards a violent and authoritarian new ruling élite. Non-violent action as a policy and as a technique avoids these problems; its means reflect its ends. With non-violent action, energy is aimed at policies or structures, and not their supports.[1]

Organisations trying to further their cause with violence are usually admitting that they have no hope of success, perhaps because the cause will not survive close examination. If this is the case it deserves to fail.

Martin Luther King and his non-violent civil rights movement showed what could be done in the United States. The trade union movement in the early part of this century showed what could be achieved without violence to relieve the conditions of the working classes. Of course these were fairly big minorities, but the non-violent options for action are many and varied, as I hope we will see in this book, and I doubt if many groups in Britain could demonstrate that they have exhausted them all.

There is a big difference between violent protest and direct action. If a farmer is about to demolish a rare wildlife habitat with bulldozers and environmentalists need to buy time and achieve official protection for it, then they are, in my view, justified in taking direct action. *Violence* would be to pull the farmer off the machine and restrain him or her forcibly – possibly to throw stones or even tie him or her up. *Non-violent direct action* would be for the conservationists to sit in a circle around the habitat and defy the farmer to run them down with the bulldozer. Of course, there is a possibility that he or she will do so. That is the risk the non-violent protester has to take and it is one that he or she *must* be prepared to take because, unfortunately, for non-violent protesters to be ultimately effective, they must demonstrate that even in the face of violence they will a) not retreat and b) not resort to violence themselves. To retreat is to confirm in the violent the view that violence will always win. To reply with violence is to lose the moral advantage. What has frequently moved communities to be sympathetic to protesters has been the sight of their dignified, peaceful and brave resistance in the face of the violence of their opponents, or even the police, the armed forces, or others.

Direct action can, therefore, be justified in many circumstances although it becomes less effective the more it is employed and the earlier it is employed. It should always follow every possible effort to persuade by reason. It must be demonstrated to fair-minded people that the direct action is a genuine expression of total frustration at the obstinacy, unfairness and possibly the brutality of 'the system', rather than a self-indulgent expression of the impatience of protesters.

Direct action, to be defensible, should always relate to the cause itself, and wherever possible the only victims of it should be the perpetrators of the injustice. This is not always possible, but that should be the aim. Thus I have no sympathy with the protesters who destroyed a test match cricket pitch in order to draw attention to a man they felt to have been unjustly imprisoned. The test cricketers, the cricket authorities and cricket followers not only had no jurisdiction over whether the man should have been imprisoned, but probably had not heard of him. Once they did – because they found their test match ruined – their sympathy was hardly likely to be engaged. The perpetrators of the damage would no doubt argue that it achieved massive publicity and that ultimately their man was released. My reply would be that they could have achieved the same objective by some other form of direct action more related to the police, the court and the law generally.

Wherever possible, therefore, the direct action should be devised and planned so that it contains a number of ingredients:

- if possible it should be relevant to the injustice so that a clear message emerges from the action;
- it should have imagination and humour;
- it should enlist the sympathy of people, not alienate them;
- it should be non-violent;
- it should be seen to be an expression of genuine injustice, and not the first but rather the last resort;
- wherever possible it should be within the spirit of the law.

This last point brings me to a key question: is it permissible to break the law? We had a lengthy debate on this subject at FoE some years ago. Mike Smyth, a lawyer, who was one of our board members, prepared a paper on law and demonstrations. Mike explained that the law relating to demonstrations is complex and obscure. In many cases it is also extremely old. In a memo to FoE board I wrote:

> I suspect it works rather well for the authorities in the sense that there is considerable flexibility for them but little flexibility for would-be demonstrators.
>
> My own view is that the difficulty in discussing whether we should act 'within the law' is that it is a blanket phrase, and obscures the fact that in some areas the law is 100 per cent sound, and in other areas highly questionable. It is further implied that the law is an expression of the democratic will of the people in terms of the rules and regulations they wish applied to the organisation of society, when many laws are, in fact, inflicted without a mandate, probably highly unpopular, and in many cases, unnecessary. Thus the assumption by some people that 'the law' is automatically good and right and should or can be inflexibly obeyed at all times is a naive one.
>
> On the other hand, they would no doubt argue and have a point, that the alternative – that we pick and choose the laws we obey – is a recipe for anarchy. Can we choose some laws and say of those laws 'this one is an ass and we choose to disobey it' and then object if someone else chooses another law and says the same thing, even if that law is one prohibiting robbery or violence?

I then went on to argue that FoE had always recognised that an element of social organisation was required and that this involved laws. Indeed it was often campaigning for laws. Or to restrict the polluting activities of many companies by law. Thus, it had chosen to work within a society that has and needs laws and 'in my view, of the two options, either picking and choosing laws to obey, or obeying (in principle) all laws, the latter is the one we reluctantly have to accept as the only rational option'. This did not, of course, preclude opposing silly or restrictive laws or seeking to have them changed.

However, I reminded the FoE board of the flexibility the authorities themselves have when it came to laws on demonstrations. 'The fact is that police themselves tend to interpret the law differently on different occasions. In other words, at their best, they seek to act "within the *spirit* of the law".'

I argued that we should do the same. Take the law of trespass. If you or I camp or picnic on a piece of farming land without the farmer's permission, and possibly do damage to the farm, we are trespassing on his or her land. We have no reason to be there except self-indulgence. We should have asked permission. We are trespassing. Further, if we proceed on that land with destructive intent – to damage or steal or for some other destructive reason – we are trespassing. He or she has the right to engage the law. But if he or she is proceeding with tractors and so on to destroy a Site of Special Scientific Interest – either in defiance of laws and regulations or because he or she knows that steps will be taken to use those laws and regulations to stop that action – and if we go on to his or her land to sit in front of the tractors and stop him or her from that action, we are, in my view, trespassing with reasons, 'within the spirit of the law'.

I advised FoE:

> I accept there is no legal basis for this, but I believe a moral case can be made. We may ultimately be evicted and even charged with trespass, but while we may have broken the letter of the law, I do not believe we will bring on ourselves much anger from the public at large. Indeed, it seems to me that is the real test of whether one breaks the law while observing 'the spirit of the law' – what will the public reaction be?
>
> Crude this may be, but the moment we move into the phrases like 'spirit of the law' we move into flexible interpretations and of course everybody will reach a conclusion according to their prejudices. In other words, there is no way the farmer will support our position. Ultimately the police and the courts may not be able to either. But then presumably we have decided we are prepared to face any legal penalty and the real test of the matter has been whether the public will feel there is justification 'within the spirit of the law'.

I accept that this is hardly a sophisticated line of argument, and it is undoubtedly a controversial one, but it is relevant to say that as it is the same authorities who are often the perpetrators of the injustice or the wrong that the pressure group aims to change, there can be a further injustice in that the obstacles to campaigning effectively to change the policy of the authorities are the authorities' own laws.

I do believe that the crude test I suggested to FoE – the likely public response to the activity – is in fact a sound one, both because the aim must be to retain public sympathy, and because the public sense of fair play will be an invaluable guide to whether in fact it is a fair (ie justified) form of direct action.

A classic piece of direct action was the FoE demonstration in opposition to the policy of Schweppes of producing non-returnable bottles. FoE supporters all over the country collected Schweppes bottles and one day they were dumped in a colossal pile on the front doorstep of the Schweppes head office. This attracted considerable publicity, and met most of the requirements of direct action – it was 'within the spirit of the law', it was an act that only affected the perpetrator of the bad policy (Schweppes), it was imaginative and good humoured, it was undoubtedly an effective media event, and it did not alienate the public at large.

5 Be positive

Seek to be 'for' rather than just 'against'. Be positive. A proposal for constructive action is always more attractive and more likely to obtain support than solely negative thinking.

Thus, Shelter is called the National Campaign *for* the Homeless, and not the Campaign *against* Bad Housing. CLEAR is called the National Campaign *for* Lead-free Air, not the Campaign *against* Lead Pollution. It is of importance to hold out the prospect of better circumstances and to define the ultimate objective. The ultimate objective is not to destroy or defeat but rather to create and improve.

FoE always sought to offer positive alternatives. We opposed the building of a pressurised water reactor at Sizewell and the growth of the nuclear energy industry, but in the context of being *for* the positive alternative of renewable energy sources; we opposed domination by the motor car, but in the context of being *for* an efficient, safe, economic, environmentally clean public transport system; we opposed indiscriminate use of pesticides, but in the context of being *for* controlled use and integrated pest management.

Pressure groups demanding improved services or changed policies should always acknowledge the good in the other side. This was a point made in a radio interview by Lord Ennals, formerly David Ennals, who had been on both sides of the fence, in the sense that he was once the director of Mind and thus a lobbyist, but became Secretary of State for the Social Services and thus a senior political decision-maker.

> I think that if a pressure group has had some success in a campaign it must show some appreciation of what the authorities have done. As a minister, I sometimes found that I had gone a considerable way towards what a voluntary organisation had asked for, but it didn't say thank you. It just jumped that hurdle and said 'Right, Minister, the next think you are going to do is this.' Now that can be very irritating because it is the minister who actually takes the decision. And part of the whole process is to get the minister in the receptive mood, not only to accept part of what you say, but to go on later and finally accept all of what you say.

Surely it is better to approach someone you wish to persuade on the basis of 'I admire what you have done ... I broadly support your policies ... but I would like to propose that a positive next step would be such and such ...'. Surely this is better than to approach on the lines of 'What is wrong with you? Why don't you do such and such? Are we the only people who care?' I am not advocating a show of weakness, or unnecessary flattery ... just that one should be positive about what people have done as well as critical of what they have not.

6 REMEMBER WHO THE ENEMY IS

It is rare that an organisation's objectives are furthered by the use of one second of time, one penny of money or one ounce of energy in trying to compete with, undermine or negate the activities of organisations on the same side. Such behaviour suggests a complete lack of perspective and lack of genuine concern for the issue.

One of the worst aspects of voluntary activity in Britain is the lack of co-operation and sometimes downright hostility between different groups. Wasted energy and emotion in rivalries between organisations, and wasted resources in duplication of effort and lack of co-operation, are unforgivable.

I have always tried to create coalitions of organisations and it is always exciting and reassuring when organisations sit around a table and agree to co-operate to deal with a particular problem. Remember who the real enemy is; don't waste your ammunition firing on your own side.

7 BE PROFESSIONAL

The more amateur you are, the more professional you have to appear to be. Your opponents will often try to go for the player rather than the ball; if they can point to errors or sloppy print material or disorganisation to undermine your credibility, they will.

You won't be judged just on the logic of your arguments; how you present them will matter too. The fewer resources you have, the more efficiently you will have to use them. Make it your policy to set high standards; no one expects you to do other than the best you can – but if the cause is important it *is* inexcusable to do less than your best.

It helps if you set out to build a campaign on the scale that you can manage well. Define objectives within your capability.

When we were planning the Liberal Democrat general election campaign we had to face the fact that the Tories would spend ten times and Labour five times what we had to spend. So we decided that our policy would be to do a few things well – to concentrate on the things that really mattered and achieve the highest professional standards. Afterwards, and despite the result, it was the general view that we staged the best campaign; it was our determination to be professional that did it.

8 CONFRONT PERCEPTIONS

Why does *The Sun* have millions of readers, unlike the *Guardian*? Because the *Guardian* is addressing in its own terms people as it would like them to be ... and *The Sun* is addressing in their terms the way the majority of people are.

The key to communication is that *if you want to be heard, people have to be ready to listen,* and they are more likely to listen if you *address them in their terms* than if you insist on addressing them in your own.

The first instinct of a bad communicator is to seek to repeat what someone says more slowly, or with more emphasis on key points, or even differently, in the belief that only if the other could understand or hear properly, he or she would see the rightness of the argument. But the initial negative response to such an approach usually reflects the fact that not only are the speaker and listener unable to reach accord on the answer, but they actually see the question differently too.

At the very least, if people perceive the problem differently from you, you have to *try to find common ground on the problem before you can hope to achieve common ground on the solution.*

Thus, putting things at their simplest, if someone doesn't think that apartheid is inherently bad, you have no possibility of reaching accord on how you should force South Africa to abandon it. Or, if you take some of my own campaigns:

> If the decision-makers don't believe that lead in petrol is damaging to health, why should they even consider tackling the problems associated with moving to lead-free petrol?

Or:

> If people believe official secrecy is beneficial to the public, what chance have you of persuading them to support a freedom of information act?

The first step towards persuading anybody to support you is to *look at the issue as they look at it ... not as you would like them to look at it.*

For instance, when we launched the Campaign for Freedom of Information, we were desperately anxious to win support in Whitehall, from civil servants and from the civil service unions and, it turned out, we gained support also from a number of former senior civil servants including two former heads of the Home Civil Service.

We tackled this by asking ourselves: What is really crucial in all this? We came to the conclusion that the information, the facts and the figures put before ministers as the background to a decision needed to be available, open to surveillance and open to challenge and question. How an individual civil servant then advised a minister seemed to us of no major importance. After all, the minister must publicly defend his or her decision on the basis of the facts available – and those facts would be available to us too.

Second, we acknowledged that no system could operate effectively if there was not an opportunity for people to share opinions and to debate pros and cons informally and in some privacy. We decided, therefore, that as a campaign we had no difficulty in exempting from our FoI proposals the advice given to ministers by their civil servants. The moment we did that, the moment we showed an understanding of the concerns of the civil servants – the most critical concern of the civil service – their attitude changed completely.

They didn't immediately sweep behind us, but – and this is the key point – they began to listen to what we had to say, and we began then to make inroads into their positions on the issue. As a result we eventually achieved widespread support and also endorsement from every one of the civil service unions – including the First Division Association – and from the former permanent secretaries. We did this by addressing their main concern, the confidentiality of the advice they offered to ministers.

Addressing other people's perceptions, prejudices and vested interests may mean compromise, may mean learning to live with arguments and attitudes that you find offensive; but if you fight their every attitude, if you resist their every concern, then you make achievement extremely difficult.

It's always a good idea to consider how the person you want to convince imagines you to be – and then surprise them. The more they expect to disagree with you, the more important it is to begin by saying something they entirely agree with. If they expect you to look untidy, look neat. If they expect you to shout, whisper.

The moment you get them thinking, 'Well, I didn't expect this,' the more they're likely to start listening to what you're actually saying. After all, if their perceptions about you are being proved wrong, maybe their perception of the issue is wrong too.

Campaigners are often expected to be unrealistic and unreasonable. Show that you're realistic and reasonable. By all means campaign for the world as you want it to be – but accept that you still have to campaign in the world as it is.

9 REMEMBER – THE BIGGER THE AUDIENCE, THE SIMPLER THE MESSAGE

If you're seeking to persuade just one other individual, you can afford to get into minute detail. If you're talking to millions on television, you can't. The bigger the audience, the simpler the message must be.

Why?

Because when you're talking to thousands or even millions you're addressing people in a wide range of circumstances, with varying degrees of knowledge and with many different perceptions of the issue. You can't get to each one of them to overcome that.

That's why if I were producing a party political broadcast on housing I would seek to get across no more than two or three general points – namely, that there is a hell of a problem; that the others have failed; and that we are committed to solving it. If I were speaking to an audience of 300 in a hall I would seek to get across quite a bit more – maybe two or three key policies. If you and I were in the pub with time to spare I would get into more detail about exactly how we could do it. My best chance would be with you, because I could answer your questions, I could adapt my case to your level of interest and your knowledge, and I could address your perceptions.

I have seen more appeals fail, more speakers lose their audience and more causes lost because the effort was too ambitious for the circumstances than for any other reason.

10 HAVE FAITH

The history of social change in Britain is also the history of campaigning, from the Earl of Shaftesbury's campaigns on poverty to Wilberforce's campaigns on slavery to modern-day campaigns on so many issues.

If your cause is just, if you do your best, you can win. You can get results.

I know – because, as the case histories in this book show, I have seen it happen.

Above all, never forget that every individual action helps. Every individual step in the right direction counts.

I remember when Terry Waite returned after five years' imprisonment in appalling circumstances, he told the story of a postcard that somehow got through to him after four years without any previous word from the outside world:

> One day out of the blue a guard came with a postcard. It was a postcard showing a stained-glass window ... a picture of John Bunyan in jail.
>
> And I turned the card over and there was a message from someone I didn't know simply saying, 'We remember. We shall not forget ...'
>
> That thought sent me back to the marvellous work of Amnesty International and their letter-writing campaigns, and I would say:
>
> Never despise those simple actions.
>
> Something, somewhere will get through to the people you're concerned about – as it got through to me eventually.

That was moving testimony to the fact that even the simplest contribution can made a difference.

REFERENCE

1 Brian Martin, *Changing the Cogs*, FoE Australia, 1979.

Part Two

The Practice

2 The A to Z of Public Advocacy

... national campaigns

(First published in *Pressure*)

A

ADVERTISING

At the time Shelter was launched in the mid-1960s it was possible to obtain a worthwhile return – often as much as £4–£5 for every £1 spent – from advertising in newspapers such as the *Guardian*, *The Times*, *The Observer* and so on, as well as in religious newspapers such as the *Catholic Herald*, the *Church of England Newspaper* and *Church Times*. Unfortunately, the cost of advertising has risen astronomically and yet the sum of money that donors send in response to advertising has remained more or less the same. Inflation has not affected charity donations. The person who gave £5 to charity in 1966 probably would still give £5 in 1989. Thus advertising for funds is rarely any longer a profitable exercise.

This does not rule out advertising altogether, however, for there are still occasions when it can have value.

- First, if it is timed to exploit an opportunity, such as a major television documentary on the subject of your campaign or some other event that is likely to attract a higher response than you would normally expect.
- Second, if you are having a 'week' (ie Mental Handicap Week, or Shelter Week or whatever) during which local groups all over the country are undertaking activities, and some shrewdly positioned advertising will reinforce their efforts and contribute to the success of the week.
- Third, if your campaign is planning a major drive and you feel the best way to convey your message to the most people is by a well-timed ad in a magazine like the *New Statesman* or *The Spectator*, or in a specialist magazine.

CLEAR took the exceptional step of booking a full-page ad in *The Observer* to climax the launch of its campaign early in 1982. The ad was intended to hammer home the message of the campaign. We emphasised in it that we hoped readers would contribute to its cost, and in fact the immediate return, plus the return from a second appeal to the same people later in the year, did more than cover the cost of the ad. Of greater importance, it meant a revival of interest by radio and television programmes and thousands of pounds of additional free publicity. We repeated the exercise with PaT. These were, however, gambles, albeit ones that paid off, and I would not necessarily recommend such an action.

The Police Federation achieved a major coup with an ad at a time when they were having difficulty over a pay rise. They placed advertising in national newspapers showing policemen injured in riots, or maimed by criminals, with the headline 'One way to earn £40 per week!' The effect was considerable and the advertising helped them win a higher pay award.

If you plan advertising, you should consider the possibility of persuading a number of supporters to contribute to the cost of it. An 'open letter' with a lengthy list of signatories, each contributing a proportion of the cost, can also be effective

AIMS

So you want to launch a campaign. The first essential is to determine your aims or objectives. This should be done with clarity and a sense of reality. You would be surprised how many campaigns or organisations fail because they have never been clear about what they wish to achieve, or because they have fixed unrealistic objectives that predetermine failure.

The first question is:
What do we want to achieve?

The second question is:
What part of that objective is actually achievable?

Then follow:
How? When? At what cost?

Getting the answers right is the best possible start to your campaign. Let's take the CLEAR campaign to illustrate the point.

What was our objective? It was to persuade or force the government to ban lead from petrol.

What was possible? This is where the answers differed from one section of the anti-lead movement to another. At one extreme, there were those who said it could be banned within a matter of weeks. It didn't matter what the cost was – the threat to children justified action.

In determining *our* objectives, however, we took a number of factors into account:

a) We could not demonstrate that a near-overnight ban was technically possible. The countries which had introduced lead-free petrol had phased the lead out over a generation of cars (ie insisted that new cars be made to run on lead-free petrol and that lead-free petrol be available for them, whilst old cars could end their lives on leaded fuel).

b) We knew that the petroleum and car manufacturing industries would fight an immediate ban far more vigorously than they would contest a phasing out.

c) We were well aware that many influential individuals and organisations had maintained their distance from anti-lead campaigners for fear of becoming involved in what they cautiously believed to be an over-emotive or unrealistic campaign. To obtain their support we knew we had to be seen to be medically and scientifically sound, and also to be fair and reasonable about the practical problems of a move to lead-free petrol. It was essential that what we asked for should be acknowledged by everybody as attainable. While the industries did not want a phasing out of lead in petrol, they acknowledged that it could be done. Thus this demand could not be condemned as impractical.

We defined our objectives as follows:

- To demand that as soon as possible, and in any event by early 1985, all new cars sold on the UK market be required to run on lead-free petrol.
- To demand that as soon as possible, and in any event by early 1985, all petrol stations be required to have lead-free petrol available for sale to the public.
- To urge that taxation on the sale of petrol should be imposed to create a price advantage to motorists purchasing lead-free petrol.

Thus we had established clear and realistic objectives. We came in for criticism from the more extreme wing of the anti-lead movement for what they saw as an unacceptable compromise, but I believe our realism helped win the final decision to move to lead-free petrol.

If your objective is to have a by-pass for your town, then your objectives can be simply stated to the public as:

> The ... by-pass committee seeks to have a by-pass built at ... within three years because of the environmental damage caused to historic buildings, and because of the road safety hazard caused by heavy traffic on crowded streets, several of them with schools.

This brief statement succeeds in being comprehensive and straightforward. No one can be in any doubt what you exist to do and why. You want a by-pass. You want it in a reasonable time. And you want it because your children are in danger and your lovely town is being spoilt. It sounds so reasonable that your listener's sympathy will automatically be aroused.

ANNIVERSARIES

When you do your research, note all the significant dates to do with the issue. Anniversaries create good opportunities for publicity or other campaign activities or special events. For instance, on the third anniversary of the near-accident at Three Mile Island FoE made a birthday cake in the shape of a nuclear power station and got Glenda Jackson to blow out the candles. A simple enough exercise, but the photograph made a number of newspapers and contributed to keeping people aware of the hazards of nuclear energy. Centenaries, fiftieth anniversaries, one-year-afters and so on all create the opportunity for demonstrations, receptions or other activities.

I once worked on a magazine and the editor/publisher drew my attention to the fact that *The Spectator* had just attracted a lot of advertising and publicity for its 2,000th issue. 'We can do that too,' he said. 'We must have our 5,000th issue coming up shortly.' We both turned to the magazine and checked the number of the most recent issue. It was number 5,000! Oh well, you don't win them all.

B

BARNSTORMING

One technique that I picked up from studying American political campaigning is that of barnstorming. What this means is to *hit a given area to the maximum possible effect in the shortest possible time*. Just as leading politicians at election time try to achieve as much as possible in a town or city as quickly as possible before moving on to the next, we developed barnstorming at Shelter to a point where we could achieve considerable results, and we repeated the technique when we had the provincial launches of CLEAR. What we would do was to choose a city and plan a 24-hour campaign to achieve as much publicity as possible and to leave the city with a thriving Shelter group. A public meeting would be fixed for 8.00 pm. We would arrive in town about 4.00 pm. The schedule could then consist of:

4.00 pm: interview with local morning newspaper for the next day

4.30 pm: interview with local evening newspaper for the following night

(Note the order – the morning newspaper will be published first and therefore its deadline is nearer; this attention to detail is critical.)

5.00 pm: record interview to go out on the local radio stations' local news programme at 6.00 pm

5.30 pm: record television interview with one of the two local stations in order that at ...

6.00 pm: ... we can appear 'live' on the other

(They will both begin by saying that they either have you 'live' or not at all, but once you have made your decision as to which one is going to get you, the other – unless it is a busy news day – will normally cave in.)

7.00 pm: meet potential leaders of local group, local personalities, ideally the MP, leader of the council and so on at small reception

8.00 pm: public meeting (which should have been extremely well prepared and is therefore well attended)

10.00 pm: follow-up drinks or reception for those who have attended the meeting and want to remain to sign up for a local group

11.30 pm: appearance on local radio late night chat show

The following morning

8.00 am: possibly another local radio appearance

8.30 am: breakfast in hotel with some influential local people – perhaps a newspaper editor, leader of council, local church leader or whoever

9.00 am: address assembly of most important local school

(I have often done two school assemblies in a dash by car in one morning.)

10.00 am: special period with the sixth formers of the school

11.00 am: address meeting of a local women's organisation

12.00 noon: attend lunch and address the local Rotary Club.

By then the town has been 'hit' and the local group should be well launched. See also G for Groups on pages 40 to 42.

BEGINNING

One of the most frequent questions I am asked by those who plan to launch a campaign or pressure group is 'How do we begin?' As I have stated, the first step is to *establish clear and realistic objectives.* Having done that, you have to *determine the correct strategy and tactics.*

I cannot overstate the importance of planning and preparation for a campaign. We began the research and planning for the Shelter campaign in June 1966 and it was five months later that it was launched. We began planning the CLEAR campaign in July 1981 and it was the end of January 1982 before it was launched. At FoE we began with other organisations to plan a pesticides campaign early in the new year of 1982, but it was not launched for 12 months. A campaign I was engaged in for freedom of information went into the planning stage in April 1983 but was not launched until January 1984. You need time to:

- research the problem;
- settle your objectives;
- put together your organisation;
- undertake the legal work if you register as a company, or as a charity;
- prepare your initial print material, and your case;
- brief in advance those journalists, politicians and other organisations who are likely to support you.

A crucial part of this planning process is to *determine the route to the decision you wish taken.* Where does the decision lie? Is it with the local authority? Is it with government? If with government, with which ministry? Is it with a nationalised industry? Or a commercial company? Or a health authority or school board of governors? Wherever the final decision lies, that is your *target.*

Having fixed your target, you then ask: *What is most likely to influence that target?* In other words, where is the vulnerability?

You also have to decide whether there are other subsidiary targets. For instance, while the government was the main target for CLEAR, the petroleum and car manufacturing industries were subsidiary targets, for by undermining their resolution we would undoubtedly also reduce the government's.

One of the key questions to ask is whether it should be a 'corridors of power' campaign or a public campaign.

A *'corridors of power' campaign* will be chosen where there is a possibility of achieving your objective by behind-the-scenes persuasion, by pulling strings or by getting the right people to lean on the right people.

A *public campaign* is necessary where it is clear that the normal negotiating channels need to be by-passed and politicians or companies reached at the point where they are most vulnerable – where they might lose votes in the case of the former, or money in the case of the latter.

In the case of the CLEAR campaign, we considered these two options. We decided that as the government had only a matter of months before they decided on their policy of a reduction to 0.15 grams per litre, but not to lead-free petrol, there was no possibility of changing their minds behind the scenes. Furthermore, we had little influence behind the scenes, whereas the power of the petroleum and car manufacturing industries was enormous. If we tried to win by persuasion in the 'corridors of power' we would be delayed, patronised and ultimately rejected. There was no doubt in our mind that the only way to proceed was to create such a public head of steam that those in the 'corridors' were forced to find a way to change the policy.

So, to begin, you proceed logically from step to step, answering these questions:

- What are our objectives?
- Who are the decision-makers – who is the target? How should we approach them: should it be a 'corridors of power' campaign or a 'public' campaign?
- Whose help do we need to achieve our objectives?
- What research do we have to undertake?
- In what form are we going to present our case? What resources of money and skills do we need to undertake the campaign, and where can we find them?
- When is the best time to launch and where and how?
- What are the various activities we intend to undertake, over what period of time, in what order and with what objectives?

Only when all these questions are satisfactorily answered, and all the preparatory work done, are you in a position to begin.

C

COALITIONS

Given the strength of the opposition you are likely to encounter, one of the first steps in any campaign is to recruit as much support as possible. Before seeking the support of public, politicians or media, it makes sense to *accumulate as much support as you can from other organisations*. These bring with them their own memberships, branches, contacts and influence. Thus it is possible to build up a considerable constituency of support by negotiations with a relatively small number of people or organisations.

A case in point was the CLEAR campaign. Well before it was launched we had personal meetings or correspondence with a variety of organisations we anticipated would be sympathetic. Obviously the first step was to talk to those campaigns that had already been concerned with lead in petrol, the Conservation Society with its own working party on the subject and FoE. In addition we recruited the support of the Association of Community Health Councils for England and Wales, Transport 2000, the Association of Directors of Social Services, the Advisory Centre for Education, the Association of Neighbourhood Councils and the Health Visitors Association. The invitation to the opening press conference went out in the names of all these organisations and this helped to alert the media to the potential strength of the campaign. In addition, these organisations included the CLEAR print material in their mailings and this guaranteed a wider circulation than otherwise would have been the case. They also strengthened our hand in approaching others, and eventually CLEAR was supported by 20 major organisations, all invited to nominate a member to the campaign's advisory committee.

One of the effects of the coalition was to help counter the suggestion we knew our industrial opponents would make – namely that the anti-lead-in-petrol people were, as they often said, 'a small bunch of nutters'. A coalition of well-known organisations could not be brushed aside in such cavalier fashion.

Shelter also was launched by five organisations for the homeless, and this too added credence to the launch of the campaign and established it as the major organisation in its field.

The 1984 Campaign for Freedom of Information has now developed the idea of coalitions even further. At the first meeting of organisations to discuss the campaign, we laid down a number of requirements for supporting organisations: they had to contribute money, they had to be represented on one of the campaign's major committees and had to allocate a staff member with sufficient time to contribute to the campaign, they had to undertake campaigning on the same subject during 1984; and we looked to them to feed into the main campaign their knowledge and experience of confidentiality in their own field. The intention was to build up a coalition that offered more than just support and sympathy, but also a practical working force. The effect, we hoped, would not only be one major campaign, well financed and supported by other national organisations, but also a series of mini-campaigns running in concert with the main one.

PaT was another coalition, with more than 50 supporting organisations.

This coalition approach in no way undermines either the separate identities or the work of individual pressure groups, but it does help to get pressure groups working together and creates a situation where each pressure group helps and strengthens others.

The coalition approach can be used at both national and local level. I can think of virtually no cause that cannot benefit from it.

Having quoted the case of a town needing a by-pass, let's stick with it to see how a coalition could be built for a local campaign. Let's assume the moving force is a small group of townspeople who have become frustrated at the failure of their MP and the local authority. The townspeople should list the number of organisations that could be concerned: local conservation and environmental organisations, organisations concerned with children such as parent–teachers, an organisation – if one exists – of residents on the streets directly affected and so on. All the organisations should be called to a meeting to settle on a plan and nominate representatives to a central committee, but should also be invited to run a separate campaign themselves. Thus, the local authority, county council and ultimately the local MP will not find themselves dealing with only one, albeit powerful, committee on behalf of the town – although this is essential – but also with correspondence and deputations and approaches from a variety of other organisations as well. The local authority and MP should be shamed into action by all this activity by being made to feel as ineffectual as they have in fact probably been.

Remember: strength comes in numbers. *Every organisation you can involve gives your campaign greater credibility, greater influence and greater resources.*

This is of such importance that you should approach it properly. If you write letters, they must be well presented and well argued and give all the reasons a) why other organisations should support the campaign, b) why you believe you will succeed and c) what you expect of them.

Far better, however, is to meet with the key figure in the organisation and discuss it fully so as to recruit his or her individual support within their own organisation; far better that when your letter arrives at an executive meeting of the organisation, its chairperson or secretary can explain fully what the background is and argue the case.

This can take a lot of time, but the rewards are considerable.

CONTACTS

The old saying 'It doesn't matter what you know but who you know' is, like all clichés, not entirely the truth. Nevertheless *contacts with the people with the right skills or people with influence in the right places* are crucial to any campaign. Thus an early step is to list every contact that your group has – politicians, civil servants, industrialists, churchpeople, leaders of other organisations, showbusiness people, journalists – anybody at all who could be an asset.

Once you have that list, how you approach and seek to deploy those contacts is critical. Perhaps a far more useful saying would be 'It doesn't only matter who you know, but how you approach them.' *Never* approach a contact until you know exactly what it is you wish them to do. *Always* approach them with a clear request, making it as simple as possible for them.

I have often been approached by organisations who have told me of their campaign or problem. 'What do you want me to do?' I have asked them. Most times they have no answer. They have not thought of that. They have simply thought 'Des Wilson would be useful.' This simply won't do. Most people who rate being on a list of valuable contacts are there because they are busy, and effective in their fields. They may well be prepared to help but they haven't the time to think for themselves how they should help. The correct answer should be 'Well, we know you don't have a lot of time but it would be tremendously useful if you could …'. As always, you should show perspective – you should make a request that is clear and realistic, given the likely time-availability of your contact. It should be a request that is actually within their capacity to grant with the minimum inconvenience.

In approaching contacts, it is crucial that you engage their sympathy quickly, and this is not always done just by telling them of the problem. Often they are more impressed by what you are doing about it. Thus it is best to say something like:

> We are deeply concerned about the lack of facilities for the handicapped in the community. We are already raising money and have provided a mini-bus for day trips. In addition, we have persuaded the local shopping centre to create ramps for wheelchairs. Now we wondered if you could help us by …

In a few brief words you have conveyed the problem you are concerned about, and also that you are a positive force for good. It is more difficult, therefore, for the contact to refuse to help, particularly if the request is a relatively simple one.

Second, if you believe a contact has a lot to offer it is sometimes best to approach with one or two minor requests that are easily fulfilled. Once a contact has delivered the goods, you are then able to respond with genuine thanks and also by telling him or her the effect of what he or she has done. This makes the contact feel good and worthwhile and useful, and thus more receptive to a fresh approach. 'We were tremendously grateful for what you did on … occasion and the results have been invaluable. We wondered if you could possibly spare a little more time to …'.

It is often a good idea to ask contacts whether they can be listed as 'sponsors' of your campaign. The initial approach should stress what you are *not* asking:

> We know you have a record of sympathy for the disabled and other needy, and wondered if you would lend your name as a sponsor of our campaign for better facilities for the disabled in our community. This does *not* call for financial sponsorship, although of course we welcome any donations, but rather allows us to include your name among a list of public figures who we believe will encourage the community at large to become involved. I can assure you the campaign will be responsibly administered and run, and some of the key figures involved are ….

It is important to remember that if contacts are valuable to you, they are probably valuable to others. Thus they receive many approaches and many pressures on their time. The easier you make it for them to help you, the more likely they are to repeat the help.

D

Demonstrations

In any word-association test 'pressure groups' would probably be linked with 'demonstrations' more than with any other word. Yet over the years that I have been involved with pressure groups I have hardly ever organised a demonstration. In fact I can number them on the fingers of one hand. Two were really 'rallies'. At least, the first was intended to be a rally – we booked

Trafalgar Square in United Nations Human Rights Year for a rally on the theme 'Housing is a Human Right', but that day London was hit by a torrential downpour that turned roads into rivers and Trafalgar Square into a lake. Because we had issued press releases, each of the speakers made his or her contribution, albeit brief, to an audience that consisted of a number of soaked pigeons and a reporter from the *Guardian* who dutifully covered the 'rally' the following day. Shelter subsequently held its own rally in Trafalgar Square. These two occasions achieved their objective of newspaper publicity but could hardly be called demonstrations.

On two occasions as chairman of the London branch of the New Zealand organisation HART (Halt All Racial Tourists), I was involved in mini-demos when the New Zealand rugby team was in Britain prior to a planned tour of South Africa. After all attempts to meet the team and put our point of view failed, we sat down in their hotel foyer, and later we obstructed their bus on the way to the International at Twickenham. The former demo won a few paragraphs in the New Zealand newspapers, and the latter made the ITV news.

That is the sum of my demo experience. We never had one for CLEAR. This is not to say that I am opposed to demonstrations. They are a useful weapon in the pressure group's armoury. However, I do believe that demonstrations should be organised sparingly, and only when there is no alternative. The more demonstrations there are, the less they will be a noteworthy event, and the less the media will cover them. Furthermore, they become devalued and in the end an irritant rather than an eye-catcher. Finally, in terms of influence on officialdom, demonstrations are of little value and they can be counter-productive unless related to a variety of well-argued and more responsible activities as well.

The point is: anyone can demonstrate, but few can assemble a well-researched and well-presented argument and sustain it in more conventional ways.

When is a demonstration appropriate?

First, when a special opportunity arises that is directly related to the cause and where a demonstration can be seen to be relevant and justified. For instance, when the International Whaling Federation met in Brighton in 1983, FoE and other wildlife organisations arranged a number of eye-catching demonstrations outside the hall. This was calculated to remind the delegates and the media of widespread conservation concern, and calculated to back up those who were lobbying inside the conference. The opportunity only arises once a year and this is an entirely appropriate and peaceful demonstration.

On another occasion, the Environment Secretary, then Tom King, was due to meet farmers to discuss the necessity for conservation measures for some land in his constituency which FoE were particularly anxious to protect. An FoE demonstration was staged outside the hall where the meeting took place. Inside the hall King was heard to urge the farmers to accept conservation proposals and to draw their attention to the demonstration outside. 'That is but a small indication of public opinion,' he was heard to say. This was an occasion where a minister actually used a demonstration to reinforce his argument that the farmers could not act with indifference to public opinion. While the demonstration was not intended to alter the policy that King advocated, it helped him to sell it to the farmers and thus was a worthwhile exercise.

Second, demonstration is valid where all other attempts to persuade the target to listen have failed, and the demonstrators can justify their actions on the basis of legitimate frustration. (The justification for our demos when the All Blacks were in Britain was that we had sought a private and unpublicised meeting to put our points of view and had been consistently rejected. We were finally forced to draw the All Blacks' attention to ourselves in more direct ways. We would have much preferred the former.)

Third, a demonstration is valid where, unless it takes place, more moderate action will be too late. (If, for instance, a farmer intends to destroy a valuable wildlife habitat on a Saturday morning, and the pressure group hears about it a few hours before, a well-reasoned letter to the authorities is not likely to arrive in time, let alone be considered. A demonstration may just awaken the farmer to the seriousness of the action and force him or her to give it second thought.)

The rules for demonstrations should be much the same as those for direct action:

- they should be non-violent;
- they should be imaginative and where possible good humoured;
- they should be relevant to the cause and to the target;
- they should seek to win sympathy and support, and not to alienate;
- they should where possible involve public or 'respectable' personalities whose presence underlines the seriousness of the cause and makes it more difficult for opponents to say that 'they are just a bunch of troublemakers'.

A useful test of the validity of an exercise is to ask yourself, 'What is different about this event that – given the number of demonstrations that take place, and given all the other potential news stories of the day – will convince a news editor that he should devote a reporter to yours?' It is not enough to say 'Because our message is important.' That's what they all say. You have to have a convincing answer.

Let's say the necessary conditions exist for a demonstration, and you have a good idea. Don't forget the following:

- *Involve disciplined people.* Demonstrations can be ruined by over-excitable or uncontrollable people who, confronted by police or your opponents, get out of hand. Many a carefully planned and well-organised demonstration has ended up with pictures in the newspapers of one demonstrator being carted off by the police for an undisciplined violent act. You've made the papers all right, but not with your message. Indeed, the whole event could have been counter-productive.
- If it involves banners or placards, they should all convey – good humouredly if possible – your clear message and ideally the name of the pressure group. I have seen many photographs of demonstrations in newspapers and been unable to work out from the placards what the demo is about or who organised it. Not everyone stops to read the caption. If possible, the photographs of your demonstration should convey the message in themselves, and that is less the photographer's responsibility than yours.
- *Don't forget to invite the appropriate media.* Also try to have your own photographer there, so that if the media don't attend you can quickly circulate photographs of the event.
- *Consider whether it is appropriate to invite the police.* The police have become accustomed to demonstrations and are not always negative. Sometimes the presence of police adds to the sense of occasion. The police can be bit-actors in the dramas.
- *Maximise the potential of the demonstration.* Don't make it just a media event. Have brief and well-written leaflets (not excessively indignant, but instead informative) for passers-by and spectators. Have at least one or two senior spokespeople available to take part in a private briefing if the demonstration leads to officialdom trying to diffuse the situation by calling in your representatives. (Imagine, for instance, you have a demonstration outside a ministry, the minister decides to invite a spokesperson in and you have no one there who can adequately represent the case. The minister will become all the more convinced that you don't deserve attention.)
- If at all possible try to organise a demonstration that does not alienate or inconvenience people who are not directly involved.

Design

Crucial to the success of a campaign is the image that you create for it, and in particular the design of print material. If you are a national organisation, likely to produce a lot of print material, money spent on a clever designer to create the best possible image for your campaign is money extremely well spent. If you are a local organisation, or a small one without funds, then try to find a designer who cares sufficiently about your cause to donate their services.

Often your letterhead, your poster or your leaflet is the first contact that others will have with your campaign. It should:

- show that you are a campaign of substance,
- show that you are professional,
- convey a feel for the campaign.

I believe the designs that the professional Peter Davenport created for CLEAR and for the 1984 Committee met all of these objectives.

The CLEAR symbol conveyed the image of children and pollution and motor vehicles, all within the traditional symbol for a warning on the roads. All this in one simple symbol was a real achievement. The strength and clean look of the typefaces and the layout of the various pieces of print material helped to make the campaign look professional. When taken together, our print material was designed to make the campaign look substantial.

I never cease to be amazed at the poor quality of the design of many major organisations. They almost seem afraid of appearing too professional.

E

EFFICIENCY

It can't be repeated too often:

- be professional;
- work hard;
- and be efficient.

If there is one way to kill off support, it is when people write for information or offer help and they don't receive a reply. Or if someone telephones for information or to offer help, and the person who answers the phone simply doesn't know where the information is or what the potential supporter can do. It is taken for granted in commercial practice that the telephone switchboard operator is a key staff member, and that the way in which the telephone is answered can affect the whole business. Why do so many pressure groups and voluntary organisations think they are any different?

The public, as most voluntary organisations know, tend to be ultra-critical of the administration of organisations they donate to. This is sometimes unreasonable, but it is a fact of life and should be recognised. In the setting up of any organisation, make sure that you have adequate administration. There is no point in being creative and exciting and having dynamic campaigners if, when the public response comes, your administration simply cannot handle it. Telephone calls should be efficiently dealt with. Letters should be answered quickly and well. Donations should receive a receipt and follow-up material very quickly. All donors and potential supporters should be recorded and up-to-date lists kept.

One way to achieve efficient administration with minimal resources is to anticipate every kind of enquiry and have standard approaches. For instance, there were only three of us in the CLEAR office, and it was obvious that we could not send individual letters to everybody. We therefore anticipated every kind of enquiry or offer of help that we would get and prepared standard letters. We made it our target to respond to every day's post on the same day.

If you have an office and an information system, start as you intend to go on – have it well organised and keep it up to date. Good administration takes no time at all; bad administration is unbelievably time-consuming. If you deal with the post every day, if you keep the filing up-to-date by filing every bit of material every day, you avoid huge backlogs and piles of material all over the office, and also the hours you can spend trying to find letters or pieces of paper when you need them.

This efficiency should be reflected in all you do. If you have a press conference the media who attend should be impressed by the efficiency of its organisation. The way letters are written and information is provided is crucial. If MPs, for instance, write for information, they should receive it by return of post and it should be as clearly and easily presented as possible, with one sheet of paper on the top summarising what has been sent to them and where they can find what they want. This efficiency achieves two results: first, it gives the MPs what they need, and that should hopefully contribute to the campaign. Second, the efficiency impresses them with the organisation itself, and makes them more likely to be supportive, to be prepared to respond to further calls for help, or to recommend the organisation as one of authority.

People are more likely to assume a campaign with an air of efficiency is right in its demands than they are a campaign that is obviously incompetently run. Efficiency doesn't cost money. It doesn't require special talents. It requires a determination to do things properly and to put in the necessary hours.

F

FUND-RAISING

Fund-raising is the most difficult and dislikeable part of pressure group activity, but also one of the most necessary activities. No pressure group can operate without spending money and, unless you have considerable personal reserves – and this is rarely the case – it has to be raised from others. For more on this subject, see pages 115 to 121.

G

GIMMICKS

Gimmicks have their place. But they should be kept in their place.

Remember, your cause is either of substance or it is not. If it is of substance, it must be argued in a substantial way. Too many gimmicks can create the impression that you don't have a substantial case. Thus, your gimmicks should be few, beautifully timed, imaginative and if possible humorous.

Joe Weston, an FoE member living in Oxfordshire, had a brilliant idea to draw attention to the potential destruction of some historic fields at Otmoor by the proposed M40. With the co-operation of a farmer on the site, he divided it into thousands of small plots and sold them to environmentalists all round the world, from Dr David Bellamy in Britain to John Denver in Colorado, and even to people as far away as Papua New Guinea. The 'sale' of these plots of land achieved enormous publicity and at the same time created a bureaucratic nightmare because the road could not be built until negotiations had taken place with each of the owners. There is no question that Joe Weston both put a considerable spanner in the works and drew attention to the threat to Otmoor by a simple yet highly imaginative gimmick.

Groups

If you plan a pressure group on a national issue, and you expect the battle to be prolonged and require support throughout the country, then you need to think in terms of local groups.

Before you decide whether to set up your own groups, consider whether there is a national organisation of local groups that would be likely to support you and whose groups would take the issue up.

I have had experience of both approaches. Shelter set up its own groups, and at one point had over 350. CLEAR, on the other hand, became associated with FoE, and FoE offered to encourage its local groups, over 200 in all, to make lead in petrol a major issue in 1982. (In fact, a number of people where there were no FoE groups decided to set up CLEAR groups, and we ended up with 12 or so. But, on the whole, the FoE groups did all that was necessary.)

So, *you may not need your own group network – you may be able to plug into someone else's*. But if that is not possible, then you should consider the following:

- *Be clear what you want from your local groups*. Are they to be fund-raising groups? Local pressure groups? Both? And what are their precise objectives? If they are fund-raising groups, do you intend to give them specific targets? If they are local pressure groups, what do you want them to do? It is vital you answer these questions properly, because the answers will determine the kind of people you are looking for to start groups and the kind of groups you want.

- *Choose the right group leader.* The right personality is one who not only is committed to your cause but has the ability to get on with other people and encourage them to act. Such people are difficult to find. You will often find someone who is completely committed to your cause but alienates everybody around them, wanting to boss the group about and unable to get co-operation or sympathy. On the other hand, you can have someone who is a terrific personality and a lot of fun, but completely hopeless at grasping the message and communicating it effectively. The ideal local group leader will a) be committed, b) be able to bring the best out of people and c) have ideas and energy. The right organiser of a local group can achieve miracles at local level. You can tell within minutes of arriving at a meeting in a town whether the local group is organised by such a person or by a no-hoper. You can see it in the layout of the hall and the number of helpers there, and in the size of the audience. So the choice of person is important. If a number of people emerge in an area, it is worth going there to meet them and if you can recognise such a potential group leader, to encourage the others to elect him or her rather than necessarily responding to the first person who offers to be the leader.

- *Keep your groups well-informed.* Group leaders should receive a special regular briefing giving them a) up-to-date facts on the cause, b) up-to-date news on the organisation's progress nationally and c) up-to-date requests for help and support. It is vital that they feel they are cared about by you and that they feel well informed. If you are having a big national press conference to launch a new aspect of the campaign, advise the local group in advance – it is upsetting for an active and committed group leader to read in the newspapers at the same time as everyone else what your campaign is doing.

- *Don't be afraid to spend money supporting your groups* and keeping your groups well informed. That money should come back in terms of even more vigorous activity at local level.

- *Don't give groups more to do than they are capable of.* On the contrary, try to give them a set of objectives that develop in size as the group develops. If they begin with a number of simple tasks which they can easily achieve, this is enormously encouraging for them and they then feel able to take on more difficult responsibilities. If you land them with too much to begin with, they can end up frustrated and disenchanted.

- *It is vital that they believe themselves to be important to you.* The more they feel you depend on them and need them and are enthusiastic about their work, the more they will do. If they begin to feel taken for granted, they will quickly dissolve, and who could blame them?

- If you appoint one or more organisers to go round the country encouraging and stimulating groups, then you are looking for a remarkable personality. For a start, organisers have to act as a link between groups and headquarters, and this inevitably puts them in a position where their sympathies are divided. They have to convey the feelings and needs of each to the other without implying a bias one way or the other and alienating either the group or the headquarters staff. Second, they have to be able to go to an area and not only absorb any complaints, defuse them and leave the group happy with headquarters, but also leave it full of enthusiasm and rejuvenated. This takes energy and confidence and considerable personality. (If anyone knows such a person, send me their name. I have spent most of my life looking for them.)
- *Try to give your groups as much information and sense of direction as possible, but leave plenty of room for them to take decisions and to employ their own ideas.* They know their area better than you do. They know their membership better than you do. They know what they can achieve better than you. They should receive plenty of ideas and suggestions from you, and requests from you, but still have the freedom to pick and choose what they do according to their own circumstances, and also to introduce their own ideas. If they send you ideas for the central campaign, consider them carefully; even if you can't use them, respond to them positively and gratefully.
- *Try to see your groups as both a whole series of mini-pressure groups and also as a national force.* Wherever possible, they should be doing their own thing at local level when it suits them. But every now and again, if they all come together as a national force, they can be a tremendous source of strength. For instance, if every MP in the House of Commons receives two or three letters from his or her own locality in the same week, it can cause quite a ripple at Westminster. You can only organise such a concerted campaign about once a year. Likewise, if you plan a series of national events that are going to attract a lot of national publicity, and you know this well in advance, you might encourage all your local groups to have some fund-raising activity in that particular week. That way they will benefit from the stimulus of the national campaign. This requires a lot of advance planning and advance warning. Often you can produce quite cheaply national posters and leaflets which can be distributed on a nationwide basis to enhance that national effort.

So far I have talked about the organisation of local groups from a national point of view. But what if you have become committed to the work of a pressure group and have decided to form a group in your own locality? How do you go about it? This I deal with in Chapter 3.

H

HOLIDAY

Have one. Whenever anyone tells me 'I have been so busy with the campaign I haven't had a holiday for three years,' my heart sinks. If they won't take a break from it they have probably lost their sense of perspective, and if they have lost their sense of perspective, heaven help the pressure group.

HUMOUR

There isn't enough humour in pressure group activity in Britain and that's a pity. I highly recommend it.

First, it keeps you from going round the bend! Second, it can be the most effective way to make a point. Third, signs of a sense of humour can be surprisingly reassuring to others. It suggests to them that you have a sense of perspective, that you are not a fanatic, that while you may care passionately and work hard for the cause, 'you haven't lost your sense of humour'.

You can show humour with one or two cartoons in your newspaper, with the slogans on placards at demonstrations, or by the nature of the demonstrations themselves – with a few jokes or witticisms in speeches, or with light-hearted irony in articles you write or letters you send to editors.

Include too much humour and everyone will think you're mad. Add a well-judged sprinkling of humour and they will be convinced you're sane.

I

IMPOSSIBLE

Don't believe it.

J

JUSTICE

Never settle for less.

K

KILL

Don't do it. There has to be another way.

L

LAUNCH

The launch of your campaign will be a big factor in your success or failure. The way you launch the campaign will determine your credibility with the media and indicate to everybody involved whether you are likely to be a campaign of substance or not. It is necessary at the launch to:

- be able to demonstrate substantial pre-launch support;
- have first-class print material, both in presentation and content, and a well-assembled case;
- stage a press conference that is professional and gives the appearance of assurance and competence.

You will need to plan to spend a fairly high proportion of your resources on an effective launch, but if it works it will be money well spent. The following are musts:

- The invitation should go out from as many sponsoring and supporting organisations as possible, in order to indicate that this is a press conference to launch a campaign of some substance.
- If possible the press conference should be chaired by a public personality of some note.
- Choose an impressive place in the centre of London – try to arrange to have it at the House of Commons or House of Lords, or in some other such place.
- Arrange for a small 'leak' to appear in a daily or Sunday newspaper within the previous seven days along the lines of 'A major campaign is to be launched next week ...', to alert the remainder of the media in addition to those to whom you have sent invitations.
- Don't just rest on the press conference; do as much prior briefing of journalists as possible. Furthermore, arrange for parliamentary questions or

some activity in the House of Commons within the following 24 hours, and hold back a good story for release within a week in order to give the campaign momentum. The launch of your campaign with its objectives and plans is sufficient to guarantee you initial publicity; if you have a good story up your sleeve, there is no need to use it at the launch press conference. Spread your ammunition over a longer period.

- Invite representatives of all the supporting organisations and other interested parties to the launch. This will ensure you have a good crowd there and a good atmosphere of anticipation and excitement. (If your press conference is at 11.00 am, you may even think of having a reception for interested parties at 12.30 pm in order to encourage and enthuse them and make the most of the occasion. To this you could invite sympathetic MPs.) See details of the launch of CLEAR in Chapter 5, and also page 53.

LETTER-WRITING

Pressure groups write a lot of letters. *There is no point whatsoever in writing these letters unless you do it well.* A bad letter will have the opposite effect to that intended. A good letter should:

- be brief;
- be clear;
- grab the reader's attention in its opening paragraph and encourage him or her to read on;
- be precise about what it wants from the reader;
- be neat and clean and without error.

A letter that rambles, is appallingly typed and is difficult to answer is likely to be put on one side or rejected.

The ideal letter should be written in such a way that it is easy to answer: it should virtually make the decision for the reader.

Letters in response to donations or offers of help are important. I have always given considerable attention to these. When it comes to donations, it is clearly not always possible to respond to every one personally. To begin with, by the time you take into account the cost of the typing, the letter-heading, the envelope and the stamp, you could end up spending more to say 'thank you' than the value of the donation itself. Thus standard letters need to be used. If these are well designed, they can be both a standard letter and a receipt. Because this is a standard response, the letter should be written with the utmost care. Those who donate large amounts should receive a personal letter, not only expressing gratitude but also indicating to them what their donation will achieve.

Just what this can mean to an organisation is best described by an experience we had at Shelter. At that time we found that if we raised £325 in cash, this would be sufficient by the time it was added to local authority loans and improvement grants for us to buy and rehabilitate a flat for an ordinary-sized family. We received a donation of £1,000 from a generous woman. We wrote her a lengthy letter thanking her, explaining that we should be able to rehouse three families with the money and saying what this would mean to them. By return of post we received a cheque from the woman for £10,000. We wrote once more, deeply grateful, and explaining that over 30 families could be helped with this money. In addition we enclosed as much material about Shelter as we could in order to make her feel that her money would be well spent. By the time the correspondence ended, her total donation was £22,000 – or 66 families helped. All of this happened because letters showed that her contribution was recognised and invaluable. Clearly this kind of response is unusual because not many people have this kind of money, but if ever there was a reward for care in letter-writing, this was it. And don't forget – it all began with the reply to the first donation. If we had taken that £1,000 for granted, as can easily begin to happen with a big organisation, the other £21,000 would never have come.

If you are writing an individual letter, *make* it individual. Five of the six paragraphs in the letter may be standard, but the sixth at least should indicate that this letter has been written for this specific individual.

The cynic may feel that this is too professional an approach. I would respond with two points. First, I cannot say often enough that if the cause is worthwhile no other approach is satisfactory. Second, I strongly believe that the individual who takes the personal decision to donate money, or offer help to your cause, should be treated with the utmost seriousness. This is someone who cares. This is someone who is a supporter – someone who is with you in what you are doing. Your campaign should reach out to him or her with the enthusiasm with which he or she has responded to your campaign. You owe it to the donor – as well as to yourselves. One of the most exciting things about being involved in voluntary activity is to see donations and letters of help and support arrive in the post. They come often from people who can little afford them. They come from people who have listened to what you have to say, who believe in you and have put their trust in you, and believe you will spend their money or use their help well. It is a great compliment to you and a great credit to them. An enthusiastic and warm and grateful response should be a natural response.

As for all other forms of letter-writing – to those in authority, to contacts, or to others who you can believe can help – remember that letter writing:

- takes time;
- costs money;
- engages your energy;
- can be counter-productive if the letter isn't good.

For these reasons you *must* do it properly. The letter should be typed. This makes it easier to read. It should, if at all possible, be restricted to one page. And it should be neat. If you achieve this, you can guarantee that it will be read. If it is hand-written, lengthy and untidy, it could be passed on to a secretary, put aside or only half read.

It is crucial that the first paragraph engages the addressee's interest or sympathy. It should if at all possible begin with a reference to them, linking them with your cause.

> Dear ...
>
> I know that for many years you have been concerned about freedom of information, and I was most impressed by your article in .... I believe, therefore, you will be supportive of our campaign to achieve greater rights of access to information.
>
> The campaign is organised by ... and its organisers include .... Its objectives are ....
>
> We would be particularly grateful if you could help. We need ... and believe that if you ... we would achieve this objective.
>
> If this is possible, perhaps your secretary could telephone me to arrange for you to allow me 10 or 15 minutes of your time, when we could discuss our campaign more fully.
>
> Yours sincerely ...

The above letter draws the recipient in by reminding him or her of commitment in the past. It quickly conveys that this is a campaign of substance, and what its objectives are. It has sought initially a contribution that will not be difficult for the recipient ... that does not require him or her to act at all; it merely asks that his or her secretary should arrange a meeting. It would be difficult for the recipient to refuse.

Finally, I believe it of importance to answer abusive letters as well. When I was at Shelter, I received some appalling letters, usually attacking the families because they had too many children or accusing us of only helping blacks. These vicious and racist letters were often upsetting, and it was very tempting to reply, 'Listen you racist bastard, we need your help like a hole in the head ...'. The trouble with such a letter is that it would confirm the hatred and the prejudice in the mind of the writer.

My approach was to always write back as follows:

> Dear ...
>
> Many thanks for your letter. I read it with care. It does indeed illustrate the size of the task we have to create greater harmony and understanding in the community and to help all of our fellow citizens to the ideal of a decent home. I can assure you we will do all in our power to achieve that worthwhile end.
>
> With all best wishes
>
> Yours sincerely ...

M

MEDIA

Considering the central place the media have in our everyday lives, it is extraordinary how they maintain an undeserved mystique. The media – newspapers, radio and television – are businesses just like any other business. On the whole, the media will help you if there's something in it for them. That 'something' is 'a good story', whether it be a news item or feature, and, of course, the best story is a good story that is also exclusive.

Pressure groups and the media need each other. Pressure groups are the source of well-researched, controversial stories for the media and the media are necessary for the pressure group to make an impact. The best way to deal with the media, therefore, is to be businesslike and professional and try to achieve a feeling of partnership. There is no need to be subservient; on the other hand, there is every reason not to be unfriendly or hostile. Whatever you do, avoid 'the problem with this country is the media' attitude. There is, of course, some truth in it, but as a basis for partnership with the media it is disastrous. You can't change the media. You have to work with them as they are. This is possible and can be fruitful.

Perhaps the best way to avoid becoming anti-media is not to think of the media as one entity, but break them down into constituent parts. First, break them down into newspapers, radio and television; then break them down into national and local; then break them down to the sections of the media that are sympathetic to you and those that have proved a waste of time; and then break it down to the individuals whom you find are most responsive to your cause and develop a special friendship and partnership with them.

Over the years I have increasingly dealt with the media in terms of a relatively small number of individual journalists whom I have come to respect and trust and with whom it is possible to 'do business'. By this I mean it is possible to sit down with them and discuss a potential story, and make an arrangement on the timing of it and how it will be handled. This way, they obtain what they want – an exclusive in their own field. You obtain what you want – the best possible story at the best possible time in the most appropriate place.

At the same time as developing this partnership with individual journalists, I also maintain an overall media service for the pressure group, and it is possible to achieve colossal publicity for your cause if you follow a number of basic principles:

- First, as always, *it requires hard work and a highly professional approach.* Many of those who condemn the media for indifference or inadequacy have in fact been responsible for the poor coverage themselves. They haven't worked hard enough. They have communicated with the media in an inefficient and unimpressive way. And they have often lost the confidence of the media by over-stating their case, by being over-aggressive or by presentation that raises serious questions over their credibility.
- *Get to understand the media and how they work,* their needs and eccentricities.
- *Master the few fundamentals* – how to write a good press release, how to evolve and sell ideas for future articles, how to interview well on radio and television, how to organise a press conference and how to manage personal relationships with journalists.

Obviously I have been helped by the fact that I was trained as a journalist. In fact, I wanted to be a journalist from the age of 10 and still call myself 'journalist' on my passport. I have the instincts of a journalist and these, unfortunately, not every pressure group organiser can hope to have. But thought, and experience, can enable any able individual to work with the media to the advantage of their cause.

Recently it has been a practice of pressure groups not to have a press officer, but to encourage each campaigner to develop his or her own contacts with the media. This has some advantages, apart from saving the cost of a salary, the main one being that you present a number of different faces to the media and the public, which is healthy. Furthermore it is always best if the central figure – whether it be the director of the pressure group, the chairman or a specific campaigner on his or her own subject – talks directly to the media, because such a person tends to be the most knowledgeable and practised in talking on the subject and comes across with a greater sense of authority and experience. However, the top-class press officer meets this point by fielding the top personalities or the relevant campaigners to do the actual interviews, while he or she does the media planning. I believe that if a national pressure group can afford it, it should have a press officer, and even voluntary local pressure groups should appoint one of their number as press officer. This person should maintain surveillance of the media, maintain press clippings files (essential), constantly look for opportunities for new stories and features, deal with day-by-day enquiries quickly and efficiently, develop a photograph file and generally provide an efficient and professional service that will make the campaign spokesperson's life easier and more effective.

Often the specific campaigners do not have as much time as they would like to maintain links with journalists; the press officer to some extent can maintain the partnership for them. Just the same, as both chairman and director of pressure groups, I have always given the maintenance of close relations with key journalists *the* top priority. Pressure groups, particularly in the public domain, need frequent and positive coverage, and the chairman or director who won't set the time aside to do it has almost definitely got his or her priorities wrong. When those with this role complain about the media, they often fail to realise that the poor coverage is their own fault.

Returning to the press officer: this should be a full-time job quite simply because there is no end to the opportunities that can be created by someone with imagination and energy. If your cause is urgent and just, then there are a thousand stories to be written about it. And out there somewhere, on the features pages or women's pages of local and national newspapers, on the hundreds of radio and television programmes broadcast every week, there are thousands of journalists looking for those stories. The press officer's job is to bring the two together.

There is so much to be done that I simply cannot conceive of a situation where the press officer of a pressure group could ever be under-employed. One could write a whole book about the mechanics of dealing with the media, and in fact a number exist, but by far the best is Denis MacShane's book *Using the Media*. Although it is written primarily for trade unionists and workers' organisations, the advice can be adapted to all kinds of pressure groups. I shall concentrate myself, therefore, on the broad principles.

Before looking at each sector of the media in turn, let's look at some of the facets of media relations that are common to all.

Press releases

The desks of news editors are piled high with press releases. Some of them contain news of real importance. Some of them are appalling public relations garbage. Don't add to the pile unless you really believe your story is likely to survive the early morning shake-up that diverts most of these press releases into the wastepaper basket. *Your media performance should not be judged on the quantity of the material you send out, but the quantity that is published.* It is far better to send out six press releases a year containing the basis for good stories, and thus win the respect of the news desk and the reporters who may operate on the principle that 'if it comes from that pressure group it is likely to be good', than to win a reputation for besieging their office with paper, most of it of no value.

- *Keep it as brief as possible* (say all that you have to say but no more).
- *Present it cleanly.* It should be typed so it can be easily handled by the journalist who has to adapt it or rewrite it for publication.
- *Tell them what they need to know in the first paragraph.* This is essential. If you don't grab their attention with the headline and the first paragraph you have probably lost them.

Denis MacShane explains this particularly well:

> Every press release should begin with the Four Ws, and should start off by stating:
>
> What is happening;
>
> Who is doing it;
>
> Where it is happening;
>
> When it is happening.
>
> The fifth W is Why something is happening.[1]

Thus, the first paragraph could read as follows:

Friends of the Earth	Who
will dump 10,000 empty bottles	What
on the doorstep of Schweppes Ltd	Where
tomorrow morning (Saturday)	When

The Friends say Schweppes should use returnable bottles
to save the waste of a million tons of glass a year. Why

The remainder of the press release will give the details and a suitable quote from the campaign, but the opening paragraph will have caught the news editor's attention.

- *Use the maximum of fact and the minimum of opinion.* The opinion should be in a specific quote from a spokesperson for the campaign to isolate it from the facts making up the remainder of the story.
- *Don't be pompous or pretentious.* Say what you have to say clearly and authoritatively, and let the story speak for itself.
- *If you wish to send a story in advance, you can embargo it.* If this is your intention, make it clear on the press release ('Strictly embargoed until 12 midnight, Saturday, 3 April'). Only employ an embargo if it is really necessary; otherwise date the story for the day after you post it, ie if you post on 1 April, it should be dated 2 April so that it is seen to be operative and up to date when it arrives on the newsdesk.
- *Learn the basics.* You should type the story double-spaced, on one side of the paper only, with wide margins and so on.
- *Don't forget to include the name and telephone number of a contact.* If it is a good story, the newspaper will wish to develop it in its own way, and will inevitably wish to follow up your press release with its own questions. Alternatively, your opponents may seek to contradict or undermine your press release, and you have to be reachable to answer this.
- If the press release is about a lengthy speech, or a report or publication of your pressure group, the press release should summarise it briefly, pin-pointing the most newsworthy aspects. The full speech or report can then be attached if the newspaper or programme wishes to develop it further.
- *Don't send photographs to radio stations.* I know it sounds absurd, but any news editor of a radio station will tell you that he or she receives plenty of press releases accompanied by photographs. Apart from the fact that this looks sloppy, it is also an appalling waste of money. Make sure that what you mail is appropriate.
- *Ensure that your media list is comprehensive and up to date.* Compile a list of all appropriate media, broken down under different headings – daily newspapers, weekly newspapers, magazines, radio, television and so on. Make sure the list is comprehensive and in tune with your objectives and the audience you wish to reach, and make sure it is up to date. Any newspaper would tell you that it receives press releases addressed to

editors or news editors who have moved on or retired, or possibly are even dead. Don't automatically send every item to the whole list – the more you can break the list down into segments, the more you can target your press releases to where they have some chance of publication. The principle should be never to send a press release to a publication you know won't use it; not only are you wasting your valuable resources if you do that, but you may alienate the publication concerned and thus miss out when you do have a suitable item.

Press conferences

The press conference has the advantage of being an event. It implies that what you have to say will have added significance, and a newspaper or programme that decides not to send anyone to it takes the risk that it may miss a good story.

This will only apply if your pressure group has a reputation for a sense of perspective. If you organise press conferences willy-nilly, irrespective of the importance or newsworthy nature of what you have to say, you will quickly find that they are badly attended and possibly not attended at all.

- *Only have a press conference on special occasions* when you can justify it on the highest news criteria.

Although CLEAR received almost unprecedented media coverage during 1982–83, we held only four press conferences in those two years. The first was to launch the campaign in January 1982; the second was to launch our autumn campaign and a CLEAR report on local authority lead monitoring in September 1982; the third was to launch our report on lead in city vegetables in March 1983; the fourth was to launch our report on lead in paint in September 1983. Sorry, there was a fifth – the press conference to mark our success in achieving a decision to phase lead out of petrol. That took place two and a half hours after the press conference of the Royal Commission on Environmental Pollution, and one hour after the press conference by the Secretary of State; journalists simply moved on from one press conference to another.

Usually the best time for a press conference is in the morning, about 11.00 am. Keep it brief. If you have more than one speaker, then the speakers should be fully briefed on the subject-matter they should cover, and should be kept to time. The chairman of the press conference should, if they are talking too much, slip a note in front of them with a 1-minute warning.

- The journalists should be given the press releases and copies of any other documents when they arrive as some have early deadlines and may not be able to stay for the whole press conference.

- If there are likely to be radio or television interviews, you should try to have a separate room available so that these can be done quietly. Often the radio and television people will wish to do their interview before the press conference because of deadlines, and you should allow for this possibility. Clearly it makes sense to do the interviews in another room; otherwise the whole press conference hears what is said and this can create a feeling of anti-climax for the press conference.

Press enquiries

An active pressure group will receive many telephoned press enquiries. They should always be dealt with courteously and comprehensively, and the image created should be of an efficient, concerned pressure group with all the time that a journalist needs. No matter how ignorant the journalist, how lazy or even how stupid (there are such individuals), be patient and help them achieve their objective – the information they need for their story.

If you are impatient, rude, aggressive or intolerant it will quite likely be reflected in the story that is published. Whatever you do, don't divert press enquiries to a junior. Remember, if whatever is said is published it will be magnified by the number of copies that newspaper produces. If you say '500' when you should have said '50' to a reporter, that error can be read by millions of people if it appears in a newspaper such as the *Daily Mirror*. Perhaps it won't matter. On the other hand, it could be disastrous.

Feature ideas

The media have insatiable appetites. Every day they eat up every idea they can get, and the next day they need more. They never stop devouring ideas. They operate 365 days a year, 24 hours a day. Any creature with an appetite like that needs help. You can be that help. You are the experts on your own area. You know all the facts, all the victims, all the injustices and needs. The media are people businesses and you are concerned with people issues. There are, as I have said, a thousand stories to be unleashed by your campaign. The media will not dig those stories out themselves. You have to do it for them.

Always be looking for possible feature ideas for radio, television and newspapers. But remember you don't exist just to serve the media, but to work with them. Therefore, the story you will wish to sell should have two ingredients: it should be newsworthy or fascinating in its own right, but it should also serve your cause. Thus, at Shelter, we would look for feature articles that might:

- Feature the plight of a homeless family (good human-interest story for the newspapers) but also convey with a few statistics the size of the housing problem and the way that families can innocently become its victims.
- Feature an unfair eviction, thus producing a good confrontation story for the media (landlord versus tenant) but, with one or two good quotes from the pressure group, also dramatise weaknesses in the Rent Act or security of tenure provisions that enabled it to happen.
- Expose conditions in hostels for the homeless (a scandal – just what the media like) but include a number of points furthering your call for firm rules on the treatment of homeless families by the authorities.
- Feature the achievements of a local housing association, a good positive people story, especially if it can contain a family reunited because it now has a decent home. At the same time, it communicates the positive side of your work.

And so on.

In the selling of the story, it is of importance to convey to the journalist why they should do it. You must picture the feature article in your mind and describe it to them as they might write it. Professional journalists will recognise a good feature as you describe it although, of course, they may do it differently.

When you meet the journalist to brief him or her in full before he or she does the feature, this is the appropriate time to negotiate the references to the pressure group that you would like. Most journalists are reasonable. If you give them a sheet of paper with facts and figures on the national problem so that they can put the specific story in context, and if you give them one powerful quote, they will normally do all in their power to use it.

Reaction to events

Unfortunately, you don't entirely control the media coverage you receive. Often you have to react to what your opponents have said, or to announcements or events. Often you have to react to attempts to smear you. Keep calm. Remain businesslike. Deal with the matter factually.

It is no good, when a journalist telephones you to say that a minister has described your organisation as 'emotional' and issued some alleged statistics that whitewash the problem, shouting down the phone to the journalist 'The man's a bastard – how dare he?' It is far better to say:

> The minister may like to create the impression that our campaign is emotional, but unlike his statistics, ours are reliable. He says there are only twenty thousand homeless people in Britain, but of course this statistic is based on the number of homeless actually in hostels. A vast number of other families are split up, living with in-laws, overcrowded, or living in slums. We would argue the number of *genuinely* homeless is more like a million. It is deeply regrettable that the minister should attempt to play down the problem instead of facing up to the policies that are necessary to tackle it – the provision of more houses at rents that poorer families can afford.

This calm but factual answer succeeds in demolishing what the minister has tried to do without being abusive. Remember, if you respond emotionally you prove his point.

If the government has announced a major change in policy, and it is the opposite of that your campaign seeks, you may be interviewed on a radio or television news programme. At the most, they are likely to have a 15- to 30-second extract from what you say. Do not appear excessively angry or emotional. Speak firmly and clearly and make a simple point.

> Anyone who has studied the evidence of the health risk to children will be bitterly disappointed that the minister has decided to perpetuate the use of lead in petrol instead of banning it altogether. I am afraid, because the medical evidence accumulates steadily, that she will be forced to reverse this decision. Our campaign will continue with even greater vigour until that is done.

National newspapers

As I have said earlier, I have become convinced that the best way to achieve consistent and reasonable coverage in national newspapers is to develop a small list of key contacts. It is wise to try to have at least two on each newspaper, because of holidays, sickness and the possibility of one journalist being away on assignment at a key time.

- Read the newspaper carefully, for some weeks, noting the subjects covered by different reporters. You will quickly be able to work out which writers are most likely to understand your cause and be sympathetic to it. Arrange to meet them for a drink or inexpensive lunch, and seek their advice. Tell them about your organisation, the cause, what you hope to achieve and what your plans are. Discuss possible stories. Ask them if you could maintain contact. Usually, provided they respect you, they will be only too pleased to establish a relationship, for you are a likely source of stories and a reporter is only as good as his or her contacts.

- *Don't bother them or hound them.* If they write a story and it isn't published, it's not their fault. They have been beaten by the sub-editors or a busy news day. They feel as bad about it as you do. There is no point in being accusing; just be sympathetic. When you speak to them next, ask if there is any way the story can be revived, indicating that you realise there was little they could do about the earlier failure.

- If stories emerge in your particular field which do not justify a press release or press conference, but if given exclusively to one journalist become stronger, offer them to one of your contacts. This is a point worth noting: some stories are only stories because they are exclusive. A document that would not be considered newsworthy if it were sent to every newspaper becomes one if the reporter can say '... this is revealed in a document obtained exclusively by the *Daily* ...'.

- Your contacts can often help you by signalling a forthcoming story to the remainder of the media. For instance, before the launch of a major campaign I usually leak a small half-story to a contact, who is happy to do a piece on the lines of 'a major campaign to eliminate the use of lead in petrol is to be launched in Britain next week ...'. The deal has to be that they have the minimum of facts so as not to break the embargo or undermine the press conference, but at the same time have just enough to whet the appetites of the remainder of the media.

- When it comes to a major story, you have to take the decision whether to release to all the press, or just to one contact. If you believe the story will achieve widespread coverage, it is probably best to publish it in a press release at a press conference. Explain to your contacts that you are doing this. They will understand. The advantage of a friendly and honest relationship with a journalist is that you can discuss these things. If you find you can't, abandon the relationship. On the other hand, if they think you are being devious or manipulative with them, they will abandon the relationship.

- Naturally, the national newspapers vary dramatically. The thinking behind news selection for *The Sun* can be very different from the *Guardian*. There is a tendency in pressure groups to obtain publicity in *The Times* and the *Guardian* and feel a sense of achievement. This coverage is, of course, of considerable importance because these are the newspapers read by decision-makers and they have an influence out of all proportion to their readerships. At the same time, the importance of the popular newspapers is their effect on a considerable number of voters. With the popular papers, it is particularly important to try to develop useful contacts, ideally with columnists or editors of specific pages who have some extra influence.

- *Don't forget letters to the editor.* These columns offer many opportunities to communicate ideas, comments and responses to what the opposition is doing. Keep them brief, be witty if you can and make sure that they make their point emphatically. The mistake most people make is to try to cover too much ground in a letter and at the end the reader is not really clear what it is they are saying or why. Thus, if there are six points you wish to make in a letter, reduce them to just one or two – the ones you can make most clearly and that are most relevant to the news item that has sparked off the letter in the first place.

Pictures

I don't know where a picture is really worth 'a thousand words', but it can often be the best chance of getting an item published, or alternatively it can draw what would usually be an inside-page story on to the front page.

The decisions on the deployment of photographers and the publication of photographs are usually in the hands of a picture editor. It often pays to send press releases and separate letters to him or her. Picture editors need ideas, and often get forgotten. Often a photographer will turn up where a reporter doesn't, and in that way you still make the newspaper.

If the photograph you intend to circulate involves other people, ask them to sign a permission form on the lines of 'I hereby authorise the Campaign for ... to distribute for publication the photograph involving myself taken on ...'. This is an essential safeguard.

Television

Essential to working with television people is to understand that they do not care about you. This is probably the most self-centred, manipulative and ruthless profession there is. I have been dealing with television people for pressure groups for nearly 20 years and I have learned to live with them, but never to believe them.

The world of charities, pressure groups and voluntary organisations is littered with people who have been let down and become disenchanted by television programmes.

I do not intend to waste space with anecdotes, or to sit in judgement on their behaviour. Suffice it to say that we have to live with television as it is, and television news and current affairs programmes have a mortality all of their own. (They also have an extraordinary ability to justify all that they do. I doubt if they will recognise themselves in what I say, or accept a word of it. The fact is that by their own values their behaviour is legitimate). There is only one way to deal with television and that is to accept it as it is and try to achieve the best you can in the circumstances.

Usually you will first be approached by a researcher. That researcher is often the most idealistic and genuine person on the programme, but he or she has no standing whatsoever. Once the director, producer and reporter become involved, the researcher is swept aside. The researcher will no doubt paint a picture to you of a worthwhile programme, sympathetic to your cause and your organisation, and you will visualise an item on the news programme or the documentary slot, presenting your case fully and fairly and enabling your representative to make the key points, if not at length then at least adequately. That is what you would like – it is not what you will get. What television seeks to do is to hold viewers. Television assumes that most people have little intelligence or patience and thus seeks to present the argument in black-and-white terms, with eye-catching pictures and as much drama as possible.

They will drain the pressure group of every bit of information it can provide. They will try to bend you to their will, making you go to all sorts of inconvenient places in order that they can have a suitable background. (Not that it will matter, because they will still show only your face or head and shoulders so that you could be anywhere. For instance, for the lead in petrol issue I was constantly being dragged out to the sides of motorways. All you saw in the picture was my head and you couldn't hear a word. Ministers, on the other hand, insist on being interviewed in the studio or at their desks in their office. The result is that you look windswept and untidy and are shouting above the traffic, while they look authoritative and calm and important sitting in their office.) Every director sees himself as a kind of Cecil B. DeMille. The whole story can be completely changed to meet television's need for pictures rather than words.

There are some ways in which you can protect yourself with television and improve your coverage:

- If it is a nightly regional news programme *try to appear live* in the studio. That way they can't cut you to pieces in the cutting room.
- Don't let them walk all over you. If you don't like the place where they wish to film you, don't go. There is no need to be aggressive – just say firmly that unfortunately you had not realised they needed this amount of your time; you have another arrangement and therefore will have to be filmed in your office or wherever you are.
- *Don't let them put you in an undignified or degrading position.*
- *Don't feel you have to answer their questions.* Use the opportunity to make the points you wish to make. Thus:

Question: 'It has been suggested that your organisation is more concerned with publicity than results. What do you say to that?'

Answer: 'Without the publicity we could not communicate the urgency of this issue – and the issue is the risk to hundreds of thousands of children of the widespread dissemination of a known poison – a neurotoxin – in petrol. Our case is that this practice is unnecessary, it has been stopped in other countries and it can be stopped in Britain, and it should be as quickly as possible.'

In this way, you have calmly brushed aside the accusation in the question and made the point you wished to make.

- If a programme such as 'Newsnight' asks you to come to the studio early and record your interview or discussion, ask yourself why. It should be more convenient for them to have you live. There can be only two possible explanations: either they intend to cut you, or they intend to have the opposition in the studio to answer you without you being present yourself. Insist on appearing live if you possibly can.

MEMBERSHIP

Whether or not you have a formal membership of your campaign must depend on its likely duration.

If, as in the case of CLEAR and the 1984 Committee for Freedom of Information, the plan is a short, sharp campaign aimed at a relatively early success, then there is probably little point in a membership scheme and the developing bureaucracy it can cause. In these circumstances it is far better to just call those who wish to support the campaign 'supporters' and have their names on a supporters' list.

The difference between a 'member' and a 'supporter' is that the former implies some influence on the policies and decision-making of the organisation. If it is decided to have a membership, it is essential to develop a democratic structure that enables its voice to be heard. Organisations that don't do this nearly always end up in trouble.

Before you fix your membership or supporters' fees, think carefully about the number you are likely to receive and what kind of people they will be. Many organisations are afraid to set a realistic membership fee and spend more to service the membership than is received in return. Members or supporters are those who have indicated their basic sympathy for the cause and are those most likely to donate generously. It makes sense to set a realistic figure that makes it possible for you to service them effectively and makes their support a source of financial strength.

It also makes sense to set the figure in the first year at a sufficient level to hold for two or three years, for all sorts of complications are caused by increased membership fees, particularly in these days of bankers' orders and the like. Alternatively, set a rising membership fee from the start, making it clear that each year it will increase by a fixed sum.

Remember that your members or supporters are a crucial source of strength and keep them informed about what you are doing and about the progress of the campaign. This is where a campaign newspaper can be helpful (see N for Newspaper on pages 62 to 64).

Watch your membership figures very closely for any trends. The start of a drop in membership should be a warning signal that either you are not maintaining proper contact with members or servicing them properly, or that the cause is losing some appeal. If there is a sudden drop in membership, contact former members and find out why. A series of telephone calls will quickly indicate whether it is a reflection of financial circumstances, a recession or whatever, or whether there is a rising tide of discontent about your policies or approach.

Finally, as in all other aspects of your campaign, keep in mind when you plan your membership scheme or build up a list of supporters what your objectives are in doing so. If it is money you want, plan the scheme so that you can raise as much from them as possible, as painlessly as possible. If it is action in their localities, build up your membership scheme accordingly, perhaps developing it around local groups.

N

Name

The decision on the name of your campaign should not be taken lightly. Ideally it should:

- be brief;
- be positive (ie *for* rather than *against*);
- convey an image of what you want to achieve.

All of these criteria were met by Shelter – the National Campaign for the Homeless, and by CLEAR – the Campaign for Lead-Free Air.

We were unable to come up with such a straightforward solution for our campaign on freedom of information, launched at the beginning of 1984, and so decided to call it the 1984 Campaign for Freedom of Information, hoping that the link with 1984 would convey the point of the campaign and deliberately encouraging the committee to become known as the 1984 Committee (rather than the 1984 Committee for Freedom of Information).

If you have an acronym for your title (eg CLEAR – Campaign for Lead-Free Air) that's marvellous, but don't strain so much to achieve it that your title actually fails to convey in the one word what the campaign is all about.

Above all, the name should speak for itself.

NEWSPAPER–YOUR OWN

A campaign newspaper is in my view an essential – the most versatile and valuable means of communication you can have. The need for a well-designed, well-compiled campaign newspaper is simply not understood by most pressure groups, to their disadvantage. When the CLEAR campaign was being planned and I mentioned that I intended to have a campaign newspaper, one of my most senior and valued colleagues protested vigorously. It was a waste of money, he said. I responded that if we spent money on no other piece of material, we should spend money on a newspaper. Furthermore, I argued we should spend whatever was necessary to produce a newspaper of high quality. The arguments for a newspaper are these:

- The format is flexible and enables the presentation of all the information you have in a variety of different ways.
- A newspaper has enormous versatility – it can be used for propaganda, it can also be used for the presentation of relatively dull but essential facts of information, and it can be used for humour. It can be used for every kind of communications technique.
- People are accustomed to reading newspapers, and normally can assimilate information more quickly from a newspaper than they can from any other source.
- A newspaper enables the campaign to talk about itself in the third person. This is a particularly valuable aspect of this medium. While to be constantly saying 'We did this and that' sounds self-centred and sometimes boastful, a newspaper can write about the activities of 'the campaign …' as if it is offering objective, third-person reporting, which has an entirely different note.

- A newspaper can constantly be updated. It can be linked to specific campaigns and have specific themes whilst retaining the central information from issue to issue.
- A newspaper can also be the basis for the campaign's appeal to its supporters and thus a fund-raising weapon.
- A newspaper can be sent to a wide variety of organisations, and inserted in a wide variety of other organisation's mailings. Whereas another organisation would think twice to agreeing to a fund-raising appeal being included in a mailing to their supporters, they are likely to find a newspaper more acceptable, on the grounds that they are conveying to their members information, albeit with a fund-raising appeal included.

The four major campaigns I have been mainly involved with – Shelter, CLEAR, FoE, and the 1984 Committee – have produced newspapers, each of them different but each of them essential.

The Shelter newspaper was published to coincide with major appeals – at around Easter-time, at the time of the publication of Shelter's autumn housing reports, at the time of its autumn political campaign and for its Christmas appeal. Its combination of stories about the homeless, coverage of the work of Shelter and fund-raising appeal meant that it raised considerable sums of money from the campaign's mailing list as well as being the ideal piece of information to hand out to interested individuals and groups.

The FoE newspaper is given as a service to all supporters and this substantial newspaper, together with all the news it contains of FoE's works, makes supporters feel that their support is worthwhile. Once more, it is the ideal publication to hand out to people who are interested in knowing what FoE is all about.

If you plan a newspaper, there are a number of factors you should take into account:

- *It should be of the highest possible standard* in design, writing, and editing; otherwise it will be completely counter-productive. Try to recruit the help of a designer, and if you cannot obtain voluntary help, pay for it. The design of the newspaper should achieve two objectives at once: first, it should reflect the image of the organisation; second, it should *look* like a newspaper – and thus achieve the image of objectivity and urgency that a newspaper conveys. Likewise, it should be well and sharply written. The size of the newspaper should be defined by the information and propaganda you wish to convey. Don't fill it with waffle. The reader should wish to turn from page to page and be impressed by the variety and extent of the information, as well as its authority. This requires imaginative editing.

- In addition to professionalism, *the newspaper requires careful tactical thought.* Unlike an ordinary newspaper, where the aim of the exercise is impact and readability, this newspaper is designed also to achieve objectives. Every item in the newspaper should be there for a good reason – either to create greater concern about the problem, to convey the breadth and quality of the organisation's work or to stimulate help and support. The reader should put down the newspaper feeling more knowledgeable about the cause, impressed by your organisation and wanting to help.
- *Do not give the newspaper a specific date or imply regularity,* but rather *time your newspaper for when it can be most valuable.* I personally believe three or four issues a year are more than adequate: one about February to launch your early-year activities, one about May to carry the campaign across the summer, one in September to launch your autumn campaign, and one just before Christmas to raise money and tie up the year's activities. But this can be varied according to your particular cause and the most appropriate occasions for publication.

  My own view is that a few substantial newspapers are better than a lot of small ones, remembering the cost of postage and also the ability of the variety of people you want to read it to cope with a great deal of information.

O

OPINION POLLS

Professional opinion polls are expensive. Few organisations can afford them and even fewer can afford them very often. But *a well-timed opinion poll is a ploy that you should at least consider.*

In the case of CLEAR, an opinion poll proved to be a critical factor in our success. We spoke to the MORI organisation, and found that for £1,000 they would include four questions in a multi-question sample of nearly 2,000 people they did on a regular basis. We discussed at length what the questions would be, and their advice was helpful. What we wanted to discover, in a nutshell, was whether the public supported a ban on lead in petrol. The first question was calculated to find out whether they knew that lead was in petrol and that it was a poison. The second and third were calculated to find out whether they supported a ban. And the final one was intended to discover whether they were prepared to pay more for unleaded fuel. It revealed overwhelming support for CLEAR.

The question then was what to do with the poll. Operating on the basis that we could achieve the maximum exposure by offering a newspaper an exclusive (see M for Media on pages 48 to 60), I discussed the matter with *The Observer*. 'If I allow you to publish this poll exclusively on Sunday,' I asked, 'Will you run it as a front page story?' They said they would have to see it. This was fair enough, and once they did they quickly confirmed acceptance of the terms. Their reasoning was simple enough: it was a good story. In fact, I didn't realise how good a story it was until *The Observer* arrived that Sunday and I found it was the front-page lead. The BBC picked it up on the Saturday evening and ran it as the first item on the radio news. The other daily newspapers all published the results on Monday.

The opinion poll was worth thousands of pounds to CLEAR, far more than the £1,000 it cost. First, we could not have bought that media exposure for £10,000. Second, it shook the politicians and the opposition by showing the strength of our support. Both *The Observer* and the *Guardian* published leading articles drawing on the opinion poll and condemning the authorities for obstinacy. We were able to quote the opinion poll time after time to demonstrate that we spoke 'for the British people'. MPs, with an election due within a year, were not slow to get the message and it was fascinating to see our Westminster support grow.

Incidentally, I did find some money for a follow-up opinion poll nine months later. There was a minor downwards shift, reflecting that we had had a quiet two or three months, but the support was still sufficiently solid to indicate that the remarkable result of the first poll was not a reflection of a high public profile at that time.

It should be said about opinion polls that they do not necessarily need to be professionally undertaken. Local groups can organise their own opinion polls in their own area and these will often achieve considerable local media publicity and be effective in shaking the complacency of local officialdom.

If you plan to undertake a local opinion poll, however, it is essential that:

- *You design the opinion poll so that it has credibility.* Positive answers to loaded questions will impress no one. The opinion poll must be carried out with the appearance of independence and objectivity. Remember that you don't have to publish the results if you don't like them.
- *It should be a substantial sample* – sufficient for your opponents not to be able to decry it as unrepresentative.

- Like all else you do, *it should be done efficiently and professionally* and the results should be well presented.

P

PETITIONS

Another form of opinion poll is the petition. Unlike the opinion poll, however, this does not pretend to be an objective test of public opinion but rather a demonstration of support.

Personally, I think that petitions have been rather over-done and as a result the authorities tend to be less and less impressed by them. *If you plan a petition, therefore, you should try to design the operation in such a way that it cannot be easily brushed off.*

Let's say it is a local problem – the need for a pedestrian crossing near a school. An impressive petition would be one that contained the signature of *every* parent, or someone from *every* household in the surrounding streets. You could hand over to the authorities not only a huge collection of names, but also a summary sheet that states that the community is 100 per cent behind your objectives. This is extremely difficult to ignore. A huge collection of names on sheets of paper does not necessarily represent a force that has to be answered; but a list of names within a given area or constituency of people who have the capacity to organise themselves and will still be there tomorrow and the day after is a different matter.

Once you have taken the trouble to organise a petition, maximise its publicity potential. Arrange to hand the petition over to a local MP or celebrity with the media present. It is often possible to obtain local television and newspaper publicity as well as to impress those to whom you are handing the petition.

My own view is that petitions are best used on local issues, and rarely.

POLITICAL PARTIES IN OPPOSITION

If you plan a national campaign, then it is a mistake to aim to influence the government only. There are three reasons why you should seek to win over the major opposition parties:

- First, *you isolate the government politically* on the issue and, particularly on a non-major issue, this makes them *feel* isolated, look obstinate and behave as if they are on the defensive. It also undermines their confidence on the issue.
- Second, *you can obtain publicity in the process* of winning over the other major parties, and they can become enormously helpful in furthering your case at Westminster, and with the public at large.
- Third, if you fail in your immediate objective of persuading the government to act, *you have sewn up the other parties so that when eventually one or other of them is returned to power, it is committed to your objective* and thus, belatedly, you will win the day in that way.

I will describe later how we did this with the CLEAR campaign. Suffice it for the moment to say that we did, and it achieved all these objectives. First, by winning over all of the other parties, we completely isolated the government and put them very much on the defensive. Second, we achieved considerable publicity and advantage by the conversions of the other parties, one by one. Finally, they were all so committed in their manifestos that had any of them been elected to office, it would have been extremely difficult for them to do other than ban lead in petrol.

I would like to be able to say that winning the opposition parties over requires the same level of argument that is necessary to win with government, but unfortunately this is not true (not, perhaps, 'unfortunately' for the pressure group, but unfortunately for the quality of political decision-making). The opposition is motivated by its desire for power and to achieve that it has to embarrass the government. It is thus more open to pressure groups able to demonstrate that the government is vulnerable on a particular issue. I have to say that none of the then three major opposition parties – Labour, Liberal, or Social Democrat – in my view carefully studied the lead in petrol issue before committing itself. Each responded to the politics of the issue rather than the issue itself. Whether or not this is desirable, the pressure group has to be aware that this is possible. Sometimes the urgency of the cause is such that the pressure group must simply play that political game. *There is a case, however, for seeking to argue the issue in as much depth within the opposition parties as possible, so that when they come to government they are genuinely committed and not superficially committed on the issue.* For instance, on the lead issue we felt so confident of our case that we would have happily argued it at every level within the Labour Party, or within the other parties. In fact, we were never called upon to do so.

POWER

Throughout the book I have referred to the 'target' of your campaign. The target, in this context, is the individual or organisation responsible for the decision you seek. I don't employ the word for dramatic effect, but rather to emphasise that all your activities need to be targeted to apply the necessary pressure on the decision-maker or decision-makers. Activities that achieve publicity or arouse attention but do not reach the target area, or will not lead to pressure on the target area, may well be a waste of time.

In order to identify the target of your campaign, you have to identify where power lies in any given situation. There is, of course, no one answer to the question: a lot of factors influence it. If the decision is a governmental one, then there are different power centres. During the early 1980s, for instance, it was generally recognised that considerable power was exercised at prime ministerial level. In some administrations, however, the centre of power can be the Treasury and the most powerful politician the Chancellor of the Exchequer. The extent of the authority of individual secretaries of state or ministers is defined by the extent that the Prime Minister genuinely delegates. Where it is the case that the power definitely lies with individual ministries, it does not necessarily follow that the powerful figure is the minister himself or herself. Once more, this differs from minister to minister, some having a firm grasp of departmental affairs and exercising considerable personal authority, and others being little better than public relations 'fronts' for their civil servants.

The campaigner, therefore, has to undertake the necessary enquiries to establish exactly who is likely to take the actual decision in any given situation (in contrast to who may announce it or have to defend it). If power lies with the minister, then you need to decide how to apply the necessary pressure on this particular minister. This also depends on a number of factors – the minister's political vulnerability, the proximity of an election, the political potency of the subject, the position of his or her civil servants on the issue, the influence and determination of the pressure groups opposed to you and so on.

In the case of lead in petrol, the decision lay with the Secretary of State for the Environment, who delegated day-to-day handling of the matter to a junior minister. They were implacably opposed to the CLEAR campaign to begin with, not least because they had announced an alternative policy less than a year earlier and did not wish to abandon it or admit error. The proximity of an election, and the huge public support for CLEAR, made the minister vulnerable, but the lukewarm support for the ministerial position by the Prime Minister herself made him even more vulnerable than usual. Therefore our strategy was to emphasise governmental indifference to the threat to children in a period leading up to a critical election, and thus force a decision for political reasons (it having become clear that they would not be swayed by the argument itself). Sceptics argued that the issue was not sufficiently politically sensitive to worry the Thatcher administration, particularly as the administration was shown to be way ahead of its opponents in the opinion polls. However, politicians, even Prime Ministers, experience considerable insecurity prior to an election and if they can deal with potentially embarrassing problems at little cost (as was the case with the lead in petrol issue) they are tempted to do so. Throughout the campaign we judged that the junior minister, Giles Shaw, would have no ultimate influence on the question and was merely being exploited by his Secretary of State, Tom King, as a front man to take all the flack. Thus it was that a week before Tom King reversed the policy Giles Shaw was still defending it on a television programme and offering little hope of change. We deliberately concentrated our fire-power on Shaw in order to 'save the face' of Tom King, while at the same time demonstrating our potential strength.

When it comes to local authorities, some research into where power lies is particularly important because it varies from council to council. On some local authorities, the leader of the council has so much power that he or she is effectively a city boss, and is the only realistic target. On others, the leader of the council has less influence and the chairman of the particular committee is the key figure. On some local authorities, the councillors do not carry a lot of weight compared with their officials and it could be a key official you wish to influence. A chat with the reporter on the local newspaper who covers the local council and some consultation with one or two members of local political parties – and perhaps a local councillor – will produce the answer. Incidentally, don't believe the first person you speak to. It's best to talk around a bit and gradually a consensus view will emerge. If you have talked to, say, six different people and four of them have said that the leader of the council is the person, or a particular committee chairman, the probability is that this is where the power does indeed lie.

If your target is a big company, a nationalised industry or some other kind of major organisation, it is necessary to establish whether the chairman or the chief executive is the most powerful of the leading characters. Sometimes the chief executive can be conservative, whereas his or her chairman can be more bold. In these circumstances it is best to win the chairman's support before you approach the chief executive. In other organisations the chairman tends to be a highly conservative figure while the chief executive is thrusting, and in these circumstances your approach will be reversed.

In defining your target you should distinguish between who is responsible for the problem, and who has the power of decision to solve it. The aim of the exercise is to achieve change and it's the decision-makers you have to influence. Time spent establishing exactly who the decision-makers are can be time saved.

Q

QUOTES

All pressure groups should have a 'quotes' file. Everyone involved in the campaign should be on the look-out for relevant remarks made by 'targets' or by other public figures; for suitable paragraphs from official reports, books or other publications on the subject; and for any other quotes that can be deployed in articles, speeches and, above all, in print material to lend authority to the case.

One well-chosen sentence or paragraph can, if quoted at the appropriate moment or in the appropriate place, have considerable impact. I am always on the look-out for entries for the 'quotes' file and draw on it on almost a daily basis.

R

RESEARCH

So you are concerned about a problem. You are angered by an injustice. You are committed to a cause. You decide to launch a pressure group. Now ... before you go any further, *become an expert*.

No matter how committed you are, or how much you think you know, before you launch any campaign research the subject thoroughly from A to Z. You cannot lose by this and you can gain in four ways. First, if there is any possibility that you are wrong, your research may save you a lot of energy and heartache. Second, if you are right, it will throw up a considerable amount of additional information and strengthen your case. Third, the research will help you to define the possible solutions and to define your objectives and priorities. Fourth, the research will make you impregnable when you launch the campaign and the opposition opens fire. You have to be able to answer every question, be right on every detail, have anticipated every thrust of the other side – the research will help you do all this.

Before the Shelter campaign was launched, no one involved questioned either the need for the campaign or the justice of the cause. Just the same, I spent three months travelling the country from one end to another researching the problem of housing in different cities, and putting together a briefing book on housing and the homeless. From that emerged the case we were able to argue for the whole five years I was involved. From that also emerged all the themes and key phrases of the campaign.

Before the launch of CLEAR, we undertook massive research to accumulate all of the medical evidence from all over the world and details of all the actions of different countries, in order that we could present an unanswerable case. Throughout the campaign we continued the research, spending a lot of our resources on it, for we recognised that the lead-in-petrol campaign would only be won if we could convince the authorities and the nation of the seriousness of the problem and of the strength of the scientific case.

Detailed research has been a feature that has distinguished FoE from some other environmental pressure groups. On nuclear energy, pesticides, transport policy, facilities for cyclists, energy conservation, recycling of resources and many other issues, FoE has commissioned and carried out extensive research in order to add authority and greater relevance to its campaigns. Typical is the pesticides campaign; although the campaign manual produced by FoE for the Pesticides Action Network consisted of around 10,000 words, the research document that backed it up contained over 120,000 and is probably the most comprehensive document in existence on pesticide use.

In my view, the research is so important to the nature of the campaign itself, to its message and themes, that you should not even consider your objectives, targets or campaign plan – let alone the design of your material or the way you intend to put it across – until the research is complete and you are able to study it and its implications in depth. Research is not just about the information to support your case – it is also about the choice of arguments and the presentation of the case itself.

With research comes knowledge, with knowledge comes authority, with authority comes conviction and with conviction comes a greater chance of success. Whatever you do, don't economise on research.

S

SPEECHES

I am afraid I have to say it once more: *I never cease to be amazed* how people who care so much and know so much about a cause will devote so little attention to presentation. This is particularly noticeable in public speaking.

Public speaking is a necessary part of campaigning, and *it is essential that you field a team of effective speakers*. This does not require talent (although being a brilliant public speaker may do). You can perform adequately with no more than confidence and careful preparation.

As always, we begin with the following question: What is the object of the exercise? Is it to inform people who have little knowledge of the problem? Is it to inspire the knowledgeable to become involved? Is it to argue the case as an advocate? Be clear what the purpose of the speech is. I have spent many, many hours sitting on platforms listening to other speakers, and in an extraordinary number of cases they clearly have not bothered to be briefed, or have been badly briefed, on the nature of the occasion. Their speech is entirely inappropriate, either in subject or in style. Many make the same speech, irrespective of the audience or the occasion, because they feel safe with it or are too lazy to adapt their performance. All these bad performances have their inevitable result: a bored or disenchanted audience. Don't bother to make a speech unless you are determined to do it properly, and if you are you will be surprised how much it will achieve.

Points to note:

- *Get a clear understanding of the nature of the occasion*, the audience, the other speakers and what they intend to do, your own place in the function and the time at your disposal.
- First, *prepare an outline of what you intend to say*. The structure of the speech is all-important. Each point should lead naturally to the next, so that you appear to be answering each question in the audience's mind just as it arises. For instance, a basic Shelter speech for me would have consisted of:
    a) attention-grabbing introduction of how many homeless families there are in Britain and what conditions they are living in;
    b) explanation of how and why people become homeless;

c) explanation of what the authorities are doing, and where they have failed;

d) explanation of why Shelter has been set up and what it can do;

e) explanation of what the audience can do;

f) inspirational call to action.

Thus I have taken the questions that any sensible individual would ask – What's the problem? How has it occurred? What are the authorities doing about it? What can you do about it? What can I do about it? – and answered them.

- *Make sure you have a lectern and a glass of water.* Check when you arrive at the meeting whether the organisers have supplied them. They probably have not. Insist on them. You must feel comfortable, and that comes from being able to refresh yourself as you speak and having a lectern to stand behind, lean on and rest notes on.

- When deciding whether to use notes, ignore all advice from public speaking books and do what you feel you can do best. If you can speak with only a few headings, use only a few headings. If you need full notes, don't be afraid to use them, but practise using them. After many years of public speaking I still write major speeches in full, although I have practised the art of speaking from them so that few in the audience realise this is so. Don't read speeches badly or mumble them, desperately trying to follow your own unintelligible writing. This is a disaster. If you intend to read a speech, have it well and clearly typed out so that you can follow it quickly. And practise reading it interestingly.

- *Don't go on and on and on.* Although nearly every speaker begins with a joke about it being their intention not to strain their audience's patience, nearly every speaker does. Of all the speakers I have heard, and there have been hundreds and hundreds, only about 5 per cent could judge the correct length for a speech. The other 95 per cent spoke for too long. I have been listening to speeches as a journalist, as a campaigner or politician for approaching 30 years, and I have never heard a speech that was too short.

- *Don't be over-emotional.* It is possible to speak with feeling and with power without the use of excessive emotion. Excessive emotion in a speech embarrasses the audience, makes everybody feel uncomfortable and tends to undermine the authority of the rest of your speech.

- *Prepare a list of the 20 most awkward questions you could expect, and jot down one-paragraph answers.* You may not have time to refer to them on the platform, but the exercise in itself will have helped. It is no sign of weakness to be prepared for awkward questions; there are inconsistencies and weaknesses in everyone's case. That's life. There is no harm in taking care to prepare the most effective answers. Incidentally, don't be afraid to acknowledge a good point, even if it is not helpful to your case. You can gain credence with the audience with the way you handle the difficult moments. ('That's a fair question, and indeed it does appear to be an inconsistency in our case. However, what you have to take into account is … .')

- *Be friendly. Be good-humoured. And acknowledge your audience.* These people could be at home watching television, could be at the movies, could be at the pub, could be almost anywhere else except in this hall listening to you. Acknowledge that. Draw them in. They are your potential helpers.
- *Adapt your speech to the circumstances on every occasion.* No speech is quite the same because no occasion is quite the same. Think about it and adapt. For instance, if you are invited by an all-party committee of MPs to speak to them, remember they are extremely busy and also extremely bad at listening. The 30-minute speech you give to a public meeting will be hopeless. At the most take 10 to 12 minutes and put the emphasis on information. Likewise, the speech you will make to a Labour Party meeting will be entirely different from the one you make to a Conservative Party meeting. The speech you make to youngsters will be different from that you make to adults. Adapt it, vary it and make it relevant to your audience.

Your audience will respect the fact that you have taken care, have put together the best speech you can and have considered the occasion and them. They won't mind if you are not a world-class orator. That attention to detail, and your sincerity, will be more than enough. Audiences only ask that you try your best … but *do* do that.

T

TELEVISION

It is advisable to maintain close surveillance of advance television schedules; a major documentary, play or film related to your cause offers a remarkable opportunity to rally support.

Shelter was launched on a wave of concern about the homeless caused by the Jeremy Sandford drama-documentary 'Cathy Come Home'. It was shown on television on three occasions and I would put a cash-donation value on it of over £100,000, quite apart from its contribution to understanding about the problem and its help in recruiting support. The film 'Cambodia – Year Zero' made by ATV led to over £1,000,000 in donations from viewers. Granada's 'Life for Christine' helped Mind in its campaign to convey the plight of the mentally ill. The BBC's 'Edna: The Inebriated Woman' by Jeremy Sandford increased understanding of the single, elderly homeless. 'Alice – a Fight for Life', Yorkshire Television's film on a victim of asbestosis, did much to boost campaigners on the health hazard caused by asbestos. Yorkshire Television's film on the possible link between the nuclear power plant at Windscale and instances of cancer and leukaemia led to a governmental inquiry. And one can go on.

Pressure groups or voluntary organisations can benefit enormously from these television programmes, but it takes planning and it is necessary sometimes to invest some money to achieve the desired result.

For instance, if you plan a direct mail appeal for funds, clearly it makes sense for that direct mail appeal to arrive in mail-boxes the day after a television programme on the subject. As I have said, at Shelter we placed advertising in the national papers and church newspapers for the days immediately after the screenings of 'Cathy Come Home'. If you have sufficient advance warning of a suitable programme, you can arrange for local groups to hold wine and cheese evenings on the evening of the programme so they can watch it together and discuss it. At the very least you should let all your supporters know about the programme, for it will have the effect of rejuvenating their concern.

If the programme is on a campaigning subject, it can make sense to advise sympathetic MPs, and even to arrange for questions to be put in the House.

Timing

You are sitting in your office and someone comes in and hands you a piece of information. It is dynamite. It will strengthen your campaign. You reach for the phone to telephone a friendly journalist who can probably have it on the front page of the *Guardian* the following day. Now ... STOP!

I repeat – STOP!

Is this the right time?

Timing is crucial in any campaign, whether it be a military one, a political one or a pressure group one.

The best time for any action is the time when it is likely to have the greatest effect. One of the secrets of success in pressure group activity is a sense of timing – knowing just when any particular action is likely to achieve its full potential. (For an account of how a piece of leaked information can be deployed at the best possible time see Y for Yellowlees on pages 81 to 84.)

A number of factors need to be calculated. If it is a politically sensitive piece of information, you have to use it at a time when it is likely to be most politically effective. If there is no particular time when it is likely to be more effective than another, then it should be used either just prior to, or at the same time as, you plan a fund-raising (or other) activity, to reinforce the impact of the organisation overall at that time. Alternatively it can be used between already planned activities to maintain the momentum of your campaign.

If it is likely to damage your 'target' you may decide to hold it until your damaged 'target' is already virtually on the floor and then employ it as the final blow. If you know your 'target' is about to score a point on his or her side, you may decide to employ it the day before, on the day itself or on the day after to defuse the effect of the target's own campaign.

Timing comes into every consideration: the structure of your campaign, the launching of it, the holding of different activities and events – almost the second question you ask yourself after 'What are we going to do?' is 'When?' So don't *only think ideas and activities, think TIMING.*

U

UNIONS

The trade union movement in the 1990s may not be the power in the land that it once was, but it is still an ally that pressure groups should seek. These days trade unions are increasingly concerned with the quality of their members' lives, health and safety, working conditions, housing and so on. Many of them have dedicated and skilled researchers and campaigners. You should at an early stage, therefore, identify the trade unions likely to be sympathetic to your campaign.

Try if possible to avoid writing directly to the general secretary in the first instance. It is better to establish who the official is whose responsibilities are likely to cover your area, and make contact with him or her. He or she can best advise how to seek union support, including possible financial support.

- Try to have an influential trade unionist on your committee or council.
- Submit articles to trade union magazines – these have big circulations, and are read by the union leaders as well as the members.
- Seek to demonstrate how your reforms can be beneficial to union members.
- Try to avoid a request for money at your first approach; it is best to achieve the union's support for the principle and then return for money at a later date if you have to.
- In approaching the union, try to get the support of someone they will respond to – ie a letter to the union on your behalf signed by another leading trade unionist, a leading member of the union itself or even a leading member of the Labour Party sympathetic to the union as well as to your cause could be helpful.

It may be helpful if I describe how CLEAR won widespread trade union support for its campaign on lead-free petrol.

First, we knew that Clive Jenkins of ASTMS had a first-class record of concern on pollution issues and a good term in his union working on these matters. We therefore approached Clive and asked if he would be a trustee of the CLEAR Charitable Trust. He accepted the invitation. (This was a particularly courageous act as many of the employees of Associated Octel, the main manufacturer of lead additives to petrol, belonged to Clive Jenkins's union and he courted some unpopularity by his support.)

Second, we arranged that Bill Sirs, general secretary of the Iron and Steel Trades Confederation, would submit a resolution calling for lead-free petrol to the annual Trades Union Congress. As the main resolutions on economic and political matters tend to be drawn from the big unions, the smaller unions will often be open to the idea of a resolution that is not likely to come from the big ones and thus more likely to create an opportunity for their general secretary to make a speech at the congress.

We discovered that the TUC General Council met at the conference venue, Brighton, a week before the congress itself, and arranged a reception for the General Council at the conclusion of its afternoon session on the Thursday before congress. It was hosted by Clive Jenkins. On this occasion I was able to talk directly with union leaders who wished to be reassured that there would be no economic or employment effects on their particular members through the introduction of lead-free petrol.

The following week the resolution was passed unanimously at the Trades Union Congress and this achieved widespread publicity in newspapers.

Did it matter?

Yes, for three reasons.

- First, because of the publicity and attention it received.
- Second, because it made it more difficult for the commercial companies involved to use economic and employment arguments once trade unionists had indicated that they cared enough about the problem to support action.
- Third, once it became trade union policy, it was possible for CLEAR to return to trade union leaders for further support. This we did in two ways. First was a financial appeal. Second, they were asked to sign letters, either to newspapers or, in one case, to the Labour Party Shadow Cabinet, asking them to keep a supply day free for the issue. Many of the trade union leaders were co-operative and this was extremely helpful.

For the 1984 Campaign for Freedom of Information we went to the National Union of Journalists before any other union to seek their full involvement and support. We argued that our aims and those of journalism were the same – the provision to the public of all the information they were entitled to have. We won their support and this was a tremendous boost to the campaign before it was even launched.

Another pressure group, Transport 2000, dedicated to the preservation of a decent public transport system, naturally went to the rail unions for support and received it.

Unions can be helpful in other ways. For instance, their leaders are influential within their industries and can often help create opportunities for meeting people, or make personal submissions where the pressure group leaders cannot themselves achieve access to the senior industrialist concerned.

Clive Jenkins, for instance, is a man to be reckoned with in most industries and when he, during an informal chat with Sir Michael Edwards, then Chairman of British Leyland, suggested that it would be helpful if British Leyland loaned a van to CLEAR for a month for its lead-testing unit, Sir Michael indicated he would be happy to do this. A letter followed and as a result of this CLEAR was loaned a brand new van.

Trade unions can be extraordinarily bureaucratic and slow in their decision-making, and even those involved in the trade union movement will acknowledge that the unions still have many faults. They also come under many pressures and tend to be extremely busy. However, I have always found trade union leaders to be warm and sympathetic and a group who genuinely care about their members. If they can be persuaded that what you want will be helpful, they can be generous in their support.

V

VISUAL AIDS

One of the effects of the television age is that people are used to being communicated to in pictures. One way to hold your audience, whether it is at a press conference, a public meeting or in any other circumstances, is to use visual aids.

In the presentation of the CLEAR case, I found that I had to use a number of quotations from organisations and medical experts, and in order that the audience would grasp their importance and take them in I had slides made of the quotations and showed them on a screen as I read them during my speech. When this was added to slides of charts and diagrams, it became an effective slide-show illustrating rather than replacing my talk, enabling me to keep the audience's attention longer and make a greater impact.

This idea of showing the actual words on a screen was adapted from the television news programme where, when they are quoting from a speech of a politician or whatever, they often show a still picture and beside the picture the actual words. It is still, I think, a rather unusual approach, but one that I find invaluable.

We had one particular diagram that we showed often during the CLEAR campaign: it showed how over a number of years the lead in blood streams of children in New York ran almost parallel to the sales of lead in petrol. You could make that remark with as much emphasis as you wished on a public platform and not really communicate the point. The chart, however, was dramatic and made a considerable impression. It was worth having a projector and screen for that one slide alone.

A good set of visual aids doesn't cost that much and can be used frequently. It is worth sending your key group organisers a set of slides and an accompanying script. They can then take them round local meetings and it helps them enormously to communicate the case. You can even hire them out if you wish to recoup the money.

Of course, these days we live in a video age and the possibility exists now, and will increasingly exist, for pressure groups to make relatively inexpensively powerful video cassettes conveying their argument with illustration. This, too, you should consider.

W

WESTMINSTER

At the end of the day it is most likely that you will succeed or fail in the Palace of Westminster – either with the introduction of a regulatory change or a piece of legislation, or with a refusal to introduce it. In Britain today the vast majority of the decisions that pressure groups seek will be taken by government, and the Palace of Westminster is the place where these measures can be advocated, the place where they have to be debated and, in the final analysis, the place where they have to receive endorsement. See Chapter 4 on lobbying.

X

XMAS

It hardly needs saying that Christmas is a crucial time for charity appeals. It can also be an appropriate time to raise money for pressure groups less traditionally associated with compassion at Christmas.

Christmas parties or Christmas fairs can combine fund-raising opportunities with exhibitions and other propaganda activity. Or, if your cause has a particular poignancy at Christmas, you can hammer home the message in posters or advertising (for instance, the 'Christmas – you can stuff it' ads placed by Shelter in the 1960s).

Every pressure group should give some thought to how it can benefit from the heightened 'peace and goodwill' at Christmas-time. If businesses can begin in January to consider how they will exploit the Christmas tradition the following December, charities and pressure groups, with more right to do so, should have no compunction in following suit.

Y

YELLOWLEES

Pressure groups seek to establish within 'the system' and the ability to do this can be the difference between success and failure. You can't beat for sheer value the equivalent on your particular subject of John le Carre's 'mole'. However, as I pointed out under T for Timing on pages 75 to 76, to obtain the leak is one thing, to achieve its full potential another. Even the best leak can be of only minimal help if the pressure group bungles the exploitation of the information.

If you obtain a leak, a number of questions immediately arise:

- What can we achieve with this?
- How shall we handle it?
- Whom should we entrust with it?
- When should we use it?

To rush out to the first journalist is not the answer. You have to guarantee that you will get the maximum impact, at the crucial time, to the maximum effect.

To illustrate how a leak can be exploited to full effect, I intend to tell you at some length the story of the now famous Yellowlees letter.

In the planning of the CLEAR campaign in late 1981, one of our main concerns was to establish medical and scientific credibility. We knew that the industries and Whitehall would seek to destroy our credibility by implying that our campaign was over-emotional and not based on any medical evidence. We therefore accumulated as much supportive evidence and opinion as we could, but nevertheless we knew this would remain a problem. Imagine, therefore, what it meant to CLEAR when a few weeks before the campaign was launched someone walked into my office and handed over a photocopy of a letter. It was written by the Chief Medical Officer of Health at the DHSS, Sir Henry Yellowlees, to senior Whitehall colleagues, and it was in political terms dynamite. It completely vindicated our concern about the risk to health of lead in petrol. He had written:

> I am taking the unusual step of writing to you about this matter. ... A year ago ... there was a degree of uncertainty, but since then further evidence has accrued which although not in itself wholly conclusive, nevertheless strongly supports the view that:

(a) even at low blood levels there is a negative correlation between blood lead levels and IQ of which the simplest explanation is that lead produces these effects.

(b) lead in petrol is a major contributor to blood lead acting through the food chain as well as by inhalation.

... it is doubtful whether there is anything to be gained by deferring a decision until the results of further research should become available. ...

... There is a strong likelihood that lead in petrol is permanently reducing the IQ of many of our children. Although the reduction amounts to only a few percentage points, some hundreds of thousands of children are affected ... I regard this as a very serious issue.

And so on.

This, we knew, added the medical weight to our campaign that we had needed. Once we saw it we knew that if we handled this correctly, we could not lose. Naturally, the temptation was to employ it at the launch of the campaign on 25 January 1982. There is no question that by dramatically producing this letter and showing it on a screen at that press conference, we could achieve considerable effect and launch the campaign with a bang. In fact, we did not. We entered that press conference with the Yellowlees letter in our pockets and never referred to it.

At the risk of sounding immodest, I would suggest to the reader that this required considerable discipline and judgement and the sense of timing I referred to earlier. The holding back of this letter at this point was to prove vital for exactly the reasons we thought it would.

First, we knew that the launch of our campaign, because of the number of organisations involved and the strength of what we would say at the launch press conference – plus some additional medical evidence at hand – would guarantee fairly substantial publicity. We intended to follow the launch press conference in London with a series of provincial launches, and because of the nature of the topic knew we would achieve widespread radio and television publicity at local level around the country. We did not need the Yellowlees letter for the initial impact. We *would* need it, however, to answer the main charge that would be levelled – that we did not have a convincing scientific case. We decided, therefore, to hold our big gun back, open the attack with the remainder of our artillery and let the opposition fire back. When their initial ammunition was wasted, we would hit them with the big gun.

There was one other reason for holding the Yellowlees letter back. As a leak, it was an extremely good story. As an 'exclusive' to one newspaper, it clearly was a real scoop. If we held it back until after the launch, we could choose the most appropriate newspaper – perhaps one that up to now had not adequately covered the story – and negotiate the best possible terms for its publication on an exclusive basis.

The campaign was launched and the launch went according to plan. We had considerable opening publicity and the petroleum industry and the politicians hit back with just the charges we expected: that they were already doing enough, that the health evidence did not justify our campaign, that everyone should remain calm and not be impressed by campaigners operating on the basis of 'emotion'.

We were not particularly happy with the coverage in *The Times* and decided that there were two reasons why we should offer the leak exclusively to that newspaper. First, because, of course, it is a highly influential newspaper. Second, because the editor at the time, Harold Evans, was known and rightly respected for his campaigning journalism, and we felt that he would not be able to resist the combination of a scoop plus the campaigning nature of it.

There were one or two problems, however. First, because the letter had identified the mole, all we now had was a typed-out version of it. Would this typewritten sheet of paper be sufficient to convince Evans, let alone excite him? We decided that if we could not show him the actual letter, the next best thing was to show him the newspaper headlines. Therefore we had a special newspaper front page printed. The idea was to run off 2,000 copies of it and on the day *The Times* appeared to have it on every MP's desk and to circulate it to other opinion-formers.

We were in Liverpool some ten days later, while the newspaper page was being printed in London, when we decided the time had come to play the Yellowlees card. I telephoned Tony Holden, the deputy editor of *The Times*, whom I knew, and told him that I had a vital document I believed to be 'dynamite'. I said I was prepared to offer it to *The Times* exclusively, but wished to come and see Harold Evans personally. Holden knew that I was a professional journalist and not likely to make a dramatic gesture without reason. He fixed for me to meet Evans at 3.00 pm the following day.

Because of the timing of our provincial launches, I had to fly down from Manchester. I met Evans and Holden in the editor's office. They accepted without reservation that it was a major newspaper story.

What were my terms?

I said simply that I would like it on the front page, that I would like it clear that it came from our campaign, and that I would like the opportunity to write a back-up feature article putting it in its perspective within the lead controversy. These were not unreasonable terms. It clearly was a front-page story. It was only fair that the source, CLEAR, should be referred to. And a campaigning article on the subject on the same day was reasonable journalism. I did, however, have one other request. Although this was Wednesday, I wished it to be published the following Monday. The reason for this was that I needed time to have that newspaper on every MP's desk by the time they arrived back from the weekend.

The following Monday the story appeared as a front-page exclusive in *The Times*, with the full letter published on page 2 and my article opposite the leader page. The following day *The Times* published a leader calling for a ban on lead in petrol. At the same time, all the other national newspapers, radio and television took up the theme of the Yellowlees letter. Michael Foot, the leader of the opposition, and David Steel, leader of the Liberal Party, challenged the Prime Minister in the House of Commons on Tuesday. The publication of the Yellowlees letter hit the lead-in-petrol issue like a time-bomb, spread-eagling the opposition and convincing almost everybody that CLEAR's case was vindicated and action had to be taken. It was a classic case of a leaked document causing the maximum possible embarrassment. I would suggest to the reader that its impact had as much to do with the use of the letter as the letter itself.

I quote this case at length in the hope that it will encourage all pressure groups to think carefully how to use such information to maximum advantage, remembering what impact they wish to make, how to do it and, above all, *when*.

Z

ZERO HOUR

This is what we all face if we don't listen to the pressure groups for peace.

REFERENCE

1 Denis MacShane, *Using the Media*, Pluto Press, London, 1979.

3 Citizen Action

... campaigning in your local community

(First published as part of the *Citizen Action* handbook)

Imagine Smithsville: an attractive place of some 100,000 people in south-east England. Part of it is encompassed within a safe Conservative constituency; the remainder is in a more marginal seat, currently held by Labour. Local administration is shared between Smithsville Borough Council and a county council. It has its own evening newspaper, the *Smithsville Standard*, and is the base for a local commercial radio station covering the whole county.

The south east has been the least affected by the economic recession, and Smithsville is relatively prosperous. It benefits from a local farming community and from light industries, and a considerable number of its citizens commute to London daily.

A traveller, calling at one of the town's homely pubs for lunch *en route* to the south coast, would judge it to be problem free. But, under the surface, rebellion is brewing ....

THE MOTORWAY

There are plans for a new motorway to take Londoners and others to the south-coast resorts. The early plans suggest that it will cut across 'the Smithsville Downs', some hilly parkland near the town, popular for picnics and walks at the weekend. It is also suggested that it will only narrowly bypass Smithsville at one point, using up one of the last remaining pockets of land available for housing. The first news of the motorway appears in the *Smithsville Standard*. The paper publishes a short leading article demanding the urgent publication of more information, urging local MPs to put down questions in the House and suggesting that, while the motorway could be beneficial to Smithsville by reducing some traffic currently passing through the town, it should be built further away – to put it bluntly, anywhere except near Smithsville itself.

One reader who becomes particularly agitated by the news is Mrs Cathy Smith, a housewife who has published a small book of her paintings of the Smithsville Downs and who sees the possibility of a motorway ploughing across them as both an environmental disaster and a personal catastrophe. As well as painting the downs, Mrs Smith leads regular walking parties across them and loves them so much that her husband Sam, an author, often jokes that after she has passed on her ghost will haunt them for ever more. 'That day may not be far off,' Mrs Smith informs her husband, 'because they'll build that motorway over my dead body!' Clutching the *Smithsville Standard* in one hand and a walking stick in the other, she heads for the downs to plan her campaign ....

THE CIVIC CENTRE

At the same time, Brian Hunter, secretary of the Smithsville Housing Action Committee (SHAC) is pondering another report in the *Smithsville Standard*. This describes a debate in the Smithsville Borough Council about plans for a modern civic centre for the town. It would cost some £20 million and would, according to the newspaper, be an all-purpose facility that would serve the town well into the twenty-first century. Mr Hunter takes the view that the existing town hall, and other facilities of the town, are adequate and that, given the ruthless Whitehall control on local authority spending, the provision of housing for young families in the area should be a higher priority. It is bad enough that according to the *Standard* a motorway could be built on one of the few likely sites for housing; even worse that limited resources are to be spent on a civic centre. He sits late into the night, the *Standard* clutched in his hand, pondering the kind of campaign SHAC would have to launch to stop the centre being built.

THE ELDERLY

In another part of the town, a local supporter of a national campaign is considering correspondence from its London headquarters. Augustine Kirkwood, the secretary of Pensioners Action Group, has received an urgent letter from national headquarters sent to all local groups. It informs them that there has been a leak from the DSS of plans to cut back housing benefit payments to pensioners. The orders will be laid in the House of Commons in three months' time unless there is a national outcry. Mrs Kirkwood's Smithsville branch is asked to apply maximum pressure on local MPs and to help support the national campaign generally.

LIGHTING UP

That same evening Mrs Marie Sheedy is walking home from a meeting of the committee of the Townswomen's Guild. To do so, she has to walk across a corner of Smithsville Fields, the town's main park, and down a number of side streets to the bungalow she shares with her husband and teenage daughters. For the umpteenth time, she feels apprehension as she walks across the badly lit fields, and down two of the side streets where the street lighting is barely adequate. At one point she imagines she hears footsteps behind her and turns hurriedly, but sees no one. When she gets home, she says to her husband: 'This time I've really had enough. I'm going to try to get the lighting improved.' She, too, sits down to plan what she will do.

Thus, this cold November evening, as the majority of the good citizens of Smithsville retire to their beds, lights burn late in at least four homes. A rebellion is brewing in Smithsville.

Can it be done?

Is it possible that Cathy Smith can beat the transport ministry, and the road lobbies? Can Brian Hunter and SHAC force the borough council to change its plans? Can Augustine Kirkwood persuade her local MPs to help the elderly? Can Marie Sheedy gets the lights turned on?

Of course they can.

And so can you. Persuading the authorities to change their plans may not be easy – but it *is* possible.

LAUNCHING THE CAMPAIGN

It would be marvellous if we could just stroll down to the High Street and buy a campaigning machine. Unfortunately they don't exist. People are the machinery of campaigning, albeit helped by the odd typewriter and photocopier, and people do not work at the press of a button.

People need to be interested, involved and sometimes even inspired. And, if people are the machinery of campaigning, then it follows that the more people you have involved, the bigger the machine.

You should seek this involvement in two stages:

- First, invite individuals or representatives of organisations you can easily interest in the issue, or who already have an obvious interest, to form a steering committee. At its first meeting more people may be suggested. This steering committee will then organise the launch of the campaign, but only the launch.

• Second, a permanent committee should be elected by everybody who has become involved by a month or so after the launch.

As many of the decisions as possible should be postponed until the maximum number of people are involved and have elected their leaders. This can lead to some delay, but patience will be repaid, for people work much harder and more enthusiastically if they have shared in the creation of the campaign rather than being presented with a *fait accompli* about objectives and tactics and just told what to do.

It's worth dwelling on this point for a moment. It is always difficult in any organisation to strike the correct balance between the maximum democracy, requiring time to be taken for consultation and shared decision-making, and the need to 'get on with it'. In my view the balance should always be tilted toward consultation and involvement. It ensures the maximum input of ideas, the maximum credibility and the maximum enthusiasm. It should also be a guiding principle that your campaign reflects your ideal of the kind of society you wish to live in; presumably that is a democratic one.

Forming a steering committee

As I have indicated, the steering committee should take as many decisions as are necessary for the effective launch of the campaign, but leave as much flexibility as possible for final decision-making by all of those who become involved once the campaign is underway. It needs to:

- conduct the initial research;
- decide on initial objectives and initial strategy;
- organise the launch with media publicity, and probably a public meeting;
- recruit further support from which the campaign organisation is finalised.

Of course one determined individual can do all this, but there are two dangers: it's hard to believe that it will be done as well as it could be if more people were involved; and such an individual may find it hard to share decision-making once the campaign is launched and a committee is formed.

It is also probable that potential supporters will have more confidence in a campaign being organised by a number of people, particularly if some represent established organisations in the community, rather than just one individual who may be suspected of having 'a bee in the bonnet'.

It probably makes sense to make the steering committee relatively small, both for speed of movement in the early stages and in order to avoid committing yourselves to too many individuals in key roles before you have recruited further support.

Where do you find your steering committee? Probably from one or all of three sources:

- *Personal friends*, but *only* if they are affected by or genuinely concerned about the issue, or have ability and/or time to offer. If none of these apply, you could end up with an embarrassing passenger on the steering committee and probably will lose a friend.
- *Others who have already expressed concern publicly*, in letters to the local papers or in other ways. If so, they are obvious candidates for they have already taken some action themselves.
- *Representatives of organisations* likely to be supportive. You may well be considering establishing a local coalition. In any case, there will be some organisations with a specific interest in your cause who will not only be willing to be involved, but may be anxious to. (See C for Coalitions on page 30.)

Once you have put a list of names together, call an initial meeting with plenty of advance warning and after checking availability, because it really is essential that all of the steering committee are at the first meeting.

At this meeting you will need to:

- discuss the issue and what further research is required;
- assign individuals to undertake further research and fix a timetable for it;
- discuss who else should be involved at this stage and arrange to invite them;
- have a good talk around the issue, and plans for a possible campaign, taking no decisions;
- fix a date for the next meeting when the research is completed.

This agenda follows the principle that you avoid committing yourselves finally, or taking any major decisions, until you have thoroughly researched the issue. Just imagine if you have been misled, or have misjudged the issue, and those whom you assume to be your opponents make a complete fool of you on day 1! Careful research will avoid this. It will also make you more effective when you have to argue your case. And the facts you produce will help determine the way you approach the campaign, your tactics and your strategy.

<u>Smithsville Housing Action Committee</u>

<u>Agenda for first meeting on Civic Centre Campaign</u>

1 Allocation of tasks for research project on Smithsville Borough Council's plans, costs, etc.

2 Discussion of plan for contrasting report showing how much housing could be provided with the money being allocated to the civic centre.

3 Invitations to the next meeting to other organisations and individuals likely to be concerned.

4 Discussion of possible strategy and tactics for a campaign.

5 Research timetable and date for next meeting.

Up to this point you should have kept your position sufficiently open to be able to abandon the whole idea without loss of face. Provided your priorities are right, there should be no problem in doing this. Presumably you have plenty of other things to do with your time, and no wish to organise a campaign that is unnecessary, quite apart from wishing to avoid the irresponsible upheaval it could cause in the community.

That's why a full, objective discussion of the issue is necessary at your first meeting and why you should consider carefully at this first meeting whether a *new* campaign is called for at all, or whether an existing organisation or organisations could achieve the objective, given a fresh approach and an injection of new enthusiasm.

Let's assume however that you *have* researched the issue fully, and have concluded that your concern *is* justified and that a campaign *is* necessary. The second meeting of your steering committee will now need to decide where to go from here.

There are two options: either to set about creating a coalition, in which case the next step will be a full meeting of representatives of all the organisations which could form part of it; or, if this does not seem appropriate, you can organise a drive for more public support, including the official launch of the campaign.

At this point a number of initial strategic decisions are called for, although they could be revised at a later date. An early decision is whether you require a substantial public campaign, or whether you need a fairly sophisticated campaign targeted on key decision-makers. Let's say, for instance, that you are campaigning to stop the discharge into your local river of pollutants from a big factory. Clearly the first target must be the management of the factory, for if you can persuade them to take the necessary measures, you can save much work, time and money. In addition to your approaches to the management you may approach the local environmental health office, the local water authority or even the Health and Safety Executive. It is possible that by involving local organisations, local councillors and others whose names are likely to impress you can win your campaign at this stage.

If, however, you fail, then you may decide to launch a major public campaign to embarrass the company, or even inconvenience it, or affect its sales.

As a rule, the public campaign should be the last resort, so that you can say to your opponents: 'We tried to talk to you quietly, we tried to reason with you, we tried to act responsibly, but you wouldn't listen, and you wouldn't respond, so now we have no alternative but to conduct the debate with you in public.'

Thus the steering committee will wish to discuss who has the power to help you to achieve your objective, and what are the various steps that should be taken before a public campaign is launched. Assuming a public campaign is still justified, however, the steering committee should consider just what it can reasonably demand, in order to fix objectives that are fair and realistic. It should discuss the kind of image it wishes to create for the campaign, in order to instil confidence in the community and show the authorities and the media that it represents reasonable and substantial community opinion. It should also discuss plans for launching the campaign, and a timetable. A public meeting will probably be planned, also an initial media launch, either with a press conference or with a press release and briefing of local journalists.

Finally, at this stage the steering committee will wish to assign jobs:

- *Co-ordinator.* At this point this could be the chairperson of the campaign although, as I will argue later, these positions will ideally become separate.
- *Secretary.*
- *Treasurer/Fund-raiser.*
- *Support organiser.*
- *Print and publicity officer.*

If a public meeting is involved, tasks for this will need to be assigned.

By the end of the meeting, everyone should have a task to undertake, and a date should be fixed for a follow-up meeting before the launch.

Remember, the steering committee should see its role as temporary, and individuals should be encouraged not to assume they will continue in these roles after the campaign is launched, although it is likely many will.

Deciding on objectives

See also A for Aims on pages 24 to 26.

It is worth spending as much time as necessary at your early meetings deciding exactly what your specific objectives are to be.

If possible, the emphasis should be on the positive. Too many campaigns are called 'Stop the ...' or 'Ban the ...'. The very name has an aggressive, negative or truculent sound. It is much better if it can be called 'The campaign *for* ...'. A campaign *for* safe street lighting sounds far more positive and worthy of support than a campaign *against* bad street lighting.

Smithsville Housing Action Committee

Agenda for second meeting on Civic Centre Campaign

1 Report back from researchers.

2 Decision on whether to proceed with a campaign.

3 Decision on whether the campaign will be run by SHAC, or whether a new coalition will be formed.

4 Decision on whether it will be a public campaign, or a campaign targeted on key decision-makers.

5 Campaign timetable.

6 Assignment of tasks:
Co-ordinator
Secretary
Treasurer/Fund-raiser
Support organiser
Print and publicity officer.

7 Initial objectives.

8 Recording of responsibilities before next meeting, and fixing date of that meeting.

Your objectives should be realistic, for two reasons: realistic objectives can be achieved whereas unrealistic ones cannot; and unrealistic objectives will deter potential supporters.

You should also consider whether your objectives are really relevant to the issue at stake. That sounds obvious, but it is possible to conduct a campaign and win, only to find that the problem remains; or, just as bad, that the solution produces new problems. This is where research, together with sensible discussion by a full steering committee, can help by ensuring you cover all the angles.

Finally, your objectives, when stated, should clearly explain both what you want to achieve and why. Thus, rather than 'We want to stop a motorway being built across Smithfield Downs,' say 'We wish to protect Smithfield Downs from road building to preserve it as a recreational facility and as a legacy for generations to come.' The latter is more lengthy, but it answers all the questions in one sentence instead of raising them in the way that the alternative, shorter sentence does.

Building support

The more people you involve, the more likely it is that you will win. There are a number of ways to set about this:

- Each member of the steering committee should undertake to recruit at least six others to the campaign. This is a realistic target, and could turn a dozen people into over 70 within a week.
- A combing of the local newspaper files will produce names of others who have written to the newspaper, or spoken at meetings, or one way or another indicated their concern.
- A full list should be made of all local organisations, and you should consider whether or not they are likely to have a special interest in your cause.
- Local councillors, MPs, opposition party candidates and others with political ambitions in the area should be listed according to whether they are likely to be sympathetic, and then approached for support.
- Local celebrities should be canvassed, for they can be helpful in a variety of ways.
- Letters to newspapers, leaflets and a stall in the High Street on a Saturday can all help to attract support.
- A public meeting will probably be a focal point for attracting support and approaching the campaign.

There are two points to remember. First, people will want to know how they can help. The steering committee, followed by the permanent committee, must make a high priority of definition of tasks and the creation of a programme providing for everybody the opportunity to help to the extent that they wish to.

Second, as soon as possible after your initial recruitment drive there should be a meeting of all of those who have offered to join the permanent group and to be involved. If a coalition is involved, and a number of organisations have expressed interest, their representatives should be invited.

At this meeting the permanent officers should be elected. They should be as follows.

President

This is useful if there is a major personality in the area who is sympathetic, but who could not be involved actively, whose name will add substance to the campaign. The president could, perhaps, be the nominal host of a function, or sign some appeal letters, or lend his or her name in some other useful way.

Chairperson

Often the chairperson of a local group is also the co-ordinator and most active member. There is, however, a case for dividing the functions and choosing as your chairperson someone with real skill at handling meetings. He or she may not be actively involved in the campaign, but will guarantee that meetings are handled dispassionately, can be an arbiter if disputes occur and can perhaps lead deputations or undertake diplomatic tasks. The chairperson will thus free the co-ordinator to get on with tasks without at the same time having to act as arbiter. Inasmuch as the division of roles dilutes power and influence within the group, this is also desirable.

Co-ordinator

None of this is intended to undermine the importance of the co-ordinator or main driving force of the campaign. Most groups need someone who can think and act on his or her feet, who is immersed in the issue and can speak effectively for it, and who can keep a grip on the campaign as a whole – co-ordinating, encouraging, responding to events and trouble-shooting.

Very often the co-ordinator will be the initiator of the campaign. Although he or she may not always believe it, co-ordinators will normally benefit from not having to chair the group meetings, and thus being free to present plans and proposals and argue them with colleagues.

Assuming the main committee meets no more than monthly (if it is a long-term campaign this is desirable, as too-frequent meetings do not allow calm analysis of where the campaign is at, or how effective it is being), the co-ordinator may organise subcommittee meetings on different projects, such as the organisation of a public meeting or a petition. If you are the co-ordinator (and if you are reading this book, you may well be), it is essential to remember that all workers are volunteers. Somehow you have to find a way of ensuring that everybody does what they have promised to do, without your becoming accusing or dictatorial. If someone is falling behind, it is far better to telephone them and say 'I guess you have a real problem on your hands; can any of us help?' rather than 'I hear you haven't done ... yet; what the hell is going on?'

Secretary

The secretary should relieve the chairperson and the co-ordinator of the bureaucracy of the campaign by calling meetings, agreeing an agenda with the co-ordinator and chairperson, taking the minutes, undertaking basic correspondence and looking after legal matters. Like the chairperson, an effective secretary will relieve the co-ordinator/organiser to get on with the primary function of keeping the campaign driving forward.

Treasurer/Fund-raiser

It makes sense for the treasurer also to be the chief fund-raiser for the group because he or she should not only think about expenditure, but also about where the money is coming from.

The treasurer has a number of functions:

- custodian of the funds, seeing that the income is properly receipted and banked and accounted for;
- producer of budgets and fundraising targets;
- organiser of fund-raising activities, preferably with a fund-raising committee.

The person you want for this task is not someone who will put a dampener on every idea by saying 'We can't afford it,' but rather someone who will work out a realistic budget and find ways of raising the money. A positive soul is essential.

Support organiser

This person, working closely with the co-ordinator, will be responsible for building up support, developing the coalition (if this is involved), establishing lists of supporters or members, finding people to help on different projects, and generally ensuring that the workpower is there when needed.

Print and publicity officer

This individual should be responsible for organising the publicity for all the group's activities, including producing the print material.

Organising a local group

It is necessary for people who declare their support or join your campaigning group to know where they fit in. Present to them clearly the different roles being undertaken and, if possible, make it clear how they can help.

Make sure your members are kept well informed. If you are a local group of a national organisation, then the secretary or co-ordinator probably receives regular mailings from the national headquarters. Make sure this information is made available to all group members.

A regular newsletter is vital. It should say what has been achieved, what is currently being planned and how people can help, and also provide the latest facts and arguments on the issue.

Remember that people have 101 options on how they spend their time. If they are going to stay interested, they must feel wanted, be up to date on what is happening, and know that the whole thing remains worthwhile. This can be achieved by the newsletter, by regular contact and by asking them to help in a way that is practicable.

You can also lose them if you ask them to do too much. If you are launching a campaign that may well run for months or even years, it is necessary to spread your activities over the year in such a way that people can get on with their own lives as well.

If, on the other hand, you are going for a short, sharp burst, you may have to ask people to make a special effort for a few weeks. Your judgement on this is important, and if there is doubt you might even consider holding back on some of your supporters in order to draft them in if the battle looks like being a longer one than you assumed initially.

Planning and timetable

At the first meeting of the permanent committee, it is worthwhile spending some time listing every idea that every member has on how to further the cause. These can then be reduced to priorities and then to a programme of action, spread over a reasonable period of time.

The aim should be first not to make too heavy a demand on your supporters and second to organise your activities so that each builds on its predecessor and the campaign gives the appearance (and hopefully has the reality) of gathering momentum.

Here are a few key points:

- *Don't fire all your bullets at once.* Keep some of your ammunition back. Let's say your research has produced two previously unknown facts that enormously strengthen your position. You may decide only to use one of them at your launch press conference, let your opponents respond to the launch and then strike with the second fact. This gives the impression of accumulating evidence behind your case. If you produce all of your facts and all of your supporters, at the launch of the campaign, it may be hard to come up with fresh news items for the local papers and to maintain the impression of growing momentum. For instance, if you have 15 local organisations planning support for your campaign, you could announce a few at the launch of the campaign and then a further three at weekly or fortnightly intervals, so that the local media is constantly running stories on the lines of 'More support for campaign on ...'. Get each organisation to issue its own press release announcing and giving reasons for its support.
- *Make sure that your activities are timed to have the maximum impact.* For instance, if a decision is in the hands of the local authority, then a build-up of publicity and obvious support just before a local council meeting, reinforced by approaches to councillors, can have the effect of applying pressure at the time when it is most likely that the matter can be discussed and influenced by what you are doing.
- *Keep it all clear and simple.* Don't complicate your lives unduly. Put it all on paper – your objectives, your plan, your timetable and your assignment of tasks, and leave space to respond to events as they arise.
- *Try and get some fun into your campaign,* and keep a sense of humour.

The launch

The launch of your campaign is the best opportunity you will have to get maximum publicity, to establish in the minds of the community that the campaign has begun and what the issue is, and to attract support.

Usually it will consist of media publicity followed by a public meeting.

If there are a number of local newspapers and a local radio station, you may decide to have a press conference. If not, personal interviews with the local media and press releases may do. Any public meeting should ride the crest of the wave following that initial publicity.

Remember that by the time of the launch you must have:

- a well-documented case based upon detailed research;
- clear initial objectives;
- a clear idea of the image you wish to create;
- an initial steering committee that gives the impression of substance;
- evidence that you have sought to achieve your objectives in a reasonable way with the authority, company or decision-making organisation concerned.

Campaigning in a coalition

See also C for Coalitions on pages 30 to 32.

There are probably more charities, community and voluntary organisations and pressure groups per head of population in Britain than in any other country in the world. This is one reason why you should think hard before launching another one. More constructively, however, it also means that there is a potential army of well-connected and experienced people who could help you win your campaign.

Increasingly, organisations are forming coalitions to tackle specific campaigns that are not central to any one of them.

From the local library or Council for Voluntary Service, or even from the *Yellow Pages*, you can probably put together a list of all the organisations in your area. Select from that list those likely to be sympathetic and invite them to put a representative on the steering committee, and to participate in the opening public meeting. Invite them, too, to be a sponsoring organisation for the campaign.

It always makes sense to make a personal approach to the leading figure in the local organisation and talk the matter over. This will ensure that when your official letter arrives, you have somebody who can interpret it sympathetically to the committee. Just the same, your secretary should write an official letter explaining the cause, who is launching the campaign, what you hope to achieve and why it is relevant to other organisations.

In addition to adding weight to the campaign simply because they support it, these other organisations can make a financial input, or lend facilities, such as a meeting hall or printing machinery.

You should also encourage the other organisations to apply separate pressure upon the decision-makers, or issue press releases, in order to help confirm the developing momentum behind the cause.

PUBLIC MEETINGS AND PUBLIC SPEAKING

See also pages 72 to 74.

Sitting on the kind of uncomfortable chair that is invariably found in public halls, listening to someone speak – invariably at far greater length than is necessary – is not the best way to spend an evening. Whey, then, do we still organise so many public meetings, and why do they still often draw a respectable audience?

The answer, as far as the organisers are concerned, is that they remain a tried and tested way of achieving some key objectives:

- They can be the focal point for a publicity campaign.
- They can help to recruit supporters.
- They can help to test opinion on an issue.
- They can often force the authorities, or your opponents, out in the open to explain or defend their positions.

But why do people come? Usually for one of two reasons:

- There is 'heat' in the issue – it affects or interests people so much that they genuinely want to know more.
- You have a speaker who is a sufficiently well-known personality to be an attraction irrespective of the issue.

Of course, if you have a combination of both a highly controversial issue and a well-known personality you are probably on to a winner – provided, that is, that you work hard. The key to the success of public meetings is *work*.

No matter how controversial the issue, or how well known the personality, if people don't know the meeting is on it will be a failure. And no matter how many people come, if the meeting is appallingly organised it will be counter-productive. Therefore it is a mistake to see the organisation of your public meeting as a relatively small task within the overall campaign. It should be treated as a major event and maximum resources should be applied to it.

The results can sometimes be spectacular: widespread publicity, better understanding of the issue, concessions by opponents or the setting up of a substantial local support group.

The planning meeting

Your group should devote a whole meeting to planning the event. You can't do it on your own; if you don't already have a committee or group you will need to persuade at least half a dozen sympathisers to help organise the public meeting, even if they reserve their position as to whether they wish to remain permanently involved in the campaign. This planning meeting should address itself to the following questions.

What is the objective of the public meeting?

If you know exactly why you are holding the meeting, then you will know exactly the kind of people you hope will come and what you want to persuade them to do. You don't want to put a lot of effort into a meeting where you end up talking to an audience who are largely irrelevant to your cause.

If you are clear on the objective of your meeting it will also help you decide on speakers, how you will publicise it and how you will organise its agenda.

Is the issue itself a sufficient attraction, or do you need a major personality?

Ideally, of course, you want both. If you need a major personality, who are the alternatives? How can they best be approached and who will do the approaching?

Where and when?

The date may be determined by the personality. If you are in a position to do so, clearly you should offer a number of alternatives.

But that is not the only factor: the timing of the meeting could be critical. If you organise it to link up with other things that are happening on the issue, so that it is in the news and interest is high, you are likely to get a better audience. Or you may decide to organise it just prior to a key date to do with the issue; for instance, just before a council meeting or a public enquiry, or at some other critical hour for the cause.

Check what else is happening. If England is playing in the final of the World

Cup on the same night and the match is televised, it clearly doesn't make a lot of sense to organise a public meeting as a rival attraction.

If there are a number of organisations in the area you think have a special interest and are likely to be well represented, check with them that they do not have rival functions on the same night.

In summary, the three main considerations are:

- When can your personality come?
- When can it be best timed to have the maximum effect on the issue itself?
- When will the number of alternative attractions in the area (or on television) be minimal?

What will be the structure of the meeting?

This will be influenced by the objective. If it is a meeting intended to achieve publicity alone, then the main requirements are newsworthy speeches, a respectable-sized audience, and above all maximum attendance from the local media.

If the aim is to develop support and build up your group of active workers, then you will need to follow the main meeting with a subsidiary one in order to sign up those people while they are in the hall and interested.

If the aim is to bring those in authority or opponents out into the open, then the opportunity will need to be created for them to speak, and for an element of debate to take place.

Here are three possible structures.

Meeting for publicity only (and assuming that you have worked hard to get all the local media there):

- Chairperson's welcome and a brief explanation of a) who organised the meeting, b) why it has been called and c) the issues involved.
- Opening speech by you, the organiser, saying why you care about this issue, why the audience should care, what has happened so far and what you hope to achieve.
- Brief (5-minute) contributions by any other major figures from other organisations in the area who support you, saying why they are concerned and why their organisation also believes that your demands should be met.
- Contribution by main speaker.

- Collection. (Best to take it at this point while enthusiasm is high, immediately after the main speaker, and before the questions and discussion period. If possible, get someone popular in the area, who is a bright personality, to give a 2- or 3-minute pitch for money.)
- Questions and discussion.
- Brief winding-up by the chairperson, reiterating the main demands of the meeting and advising people how they can support the campaign.

Meeting to form a local group and build up support. The structure of this meeting can be similar to that above, except that after the questions and discussion period you, the main organiser, should wind up the meeting rather than the chairperson. You should announce that another meeting is going to take place. In fact, you should say that it is going to take place in five minutes' time at the front of the hall. It will only last five minutes and it is for those people who feel sufficiently concerned to contribute some of their time to furthering the cause. Its aim will be to get their names and addresses, and to fix a date for a first meeting of a local group. Urge all those who can spare a little time to stay behind and commit themselves to the group.

Meeting where opponents/decision-makers will be present. This is a little different.

- Chairperson opens the meeting, explains who has organised it, what the issues are and what the structure of the meeting will be.
- You, the organiser, or someone you have chosen, will then speak, presenting the background to the issue and explaining why you believe the audience should not accept the status quo.
- Any supporting speakers from other organisations, or people who can add further evidence to your argument, should then speak briefly.
- The chairperson should then invite your opponents, or representatives of the local authority or whatever the decision-making body is, to speak and explain their policy or defend their position.
- When they have spoken they should be invited to join the other speakers on the platform to form a panel to take questions and hear discussion from the floor (the time given to speakers should be fairly well controlled to allow the maximum possible time for the panel).
- At the end of this period, the chairperson should thank your opponents/the authorities for attending and for taking part in the discussion, and invite them to leave the platform.
- The chairperson should then invite you, as the organiser of the meeting, to speak finally, not only commenting on what has emerged from the

meeting but summing up what you would now like to happen and calling for support. In the case of this particular meeting, the collection probably will need to be taken at the end.

Who is to be chairperson?

Sometimes if you can't have a major personality as a speaker, you can get one to chair the meeting, and this serves the same purpose – giving you an 'attraction'.

However, it is vital that the chairperson is competent, for a bad chairperson can lead to a bad meeting. He or she must be able to speak clearly and well and also to control an audience, particularly if things get a bit heated.

It is of particular importance that you brief the chairperson properly. Prepare a memo which explains the exact purpose of the meeting, the structure and timing, and gives biographical notes about each speaker and any other useful information. You could even consider writing the chairperson's opening remarks.

Who will do what?

The final task of this first meeting is to allocate responsibilities to at least five people. You need:

- *Co-ordinator,* whose main responsibility is to check that all of the others are doing what they have promised, to liaise between the committee members and to organise co-ordinating/planning meetings. The co-ordinator should also be a trouble-shooter to sort out any problems that occur. This person could be the overall campaign co-ordinator.
- *Hall organiser.* This person will find the appropriate hall, negotiate its hire, arrange the necessary facilities, and see that it is set up appropriately for the meeting on the night – a kind of stage manager of the event.
- *Publicity manager.* This person is responsible for getting the audience. He or she must deal with the local media, produce and distribute posters and leaflets, liaise with other interested organisations, and generally take responsibility for filling the hall with the kind of people you want there. This person will probably be your overall campaign print and publicity officer.

Remember that one of the reasons for the meeting is to obtain publicity. It is vital that you keep in touch with the local media, and see that they actually come on the night and cover the meeting fully. Encourage them to send a photographer. If by any chance they do not, make sure that you make note of the key points, write an account of the meeting yourself and hand it in the next day. Sometimes this means sitting up late on the night of the meeting in order to do it, but it will be a pity if all the work that has been put in does not achieve its full potential, and if you miss the next edition of the local paper.

Finally, it is worth considering having a publicity demonstration in the High Street on the Saturday before the meeting. This could consist of a stall outside a friendly shop, a van with a loudspeaker travelling around the shopping streets with posters all over it, and members of your committee and other helpers going up and down the street mentioning the meeting to people and giving them a leaflet. It will all help to create the feeling that something is happening in the area that may be fun to attend.

- *Agenda controller*. This person should be responsible for inviting the chairperson and speakers, liaising with them and briefing them, welcoming them on the night and generally seeing that they are looked after.
- *Treasurer/Chief steward*. I propose combining these roles, simply because a role for the stewards will be the collection and the subsequent counting of the money. This person should be given a budget for the organisation of the meeting, and should advise the others how much they have to spend on hire of the hall, loudspeakers, leaflets, posters and so on. He or she should also be responsible for organising the collection. This person, too, may be the overall campaign treasurer.

There are two other possible organising responsibilities, depending on the nature of the meeting:

- If you expect it to be a fairly small meeting, you may decide to have refreshments afterwards, in which case you need a *catering organiser* to do this.
- You may also decide to have stalls or exhibitions. If so, you will need a *stall/exhibitions organiser*.

Once you have allocated these responsibilities, you should agree as a group what each person should be doing in some detail, and arrange periodic liaison meetings chaired by the co-ordinator.

Hall organiser

As hall organiser you will have already discussed with the planning committee the possible venues. You must choose your hall carefully, to ensure that you have one of the right size and right atmosphere.

The size is critical. It will depend on a careful judgement by the whole group on how many people you think you can attract. It should look full. Therefore

To: Bert Jones

Manager

Smithsville Town Hall

Sir

I write to confirm my booking for Wednesday, 17 July, for a meeting organised by myself on behalf of the Smithsville Downs Preservation Campaign.

I confirm the following:

1 That the rental for the Sussex Room of the Town Hall is £20 for the evening, and I enclose a cheque.

2 That the meeting will take place from 7.30 to 9.30 pm, but that we will have access from 6 pm to 10.30 pm.

3 That you will be present on the evening for the opening of the hall, for practical assistance, and for the closing of the hall.

4 That we will wish to make use of the town hall amplification facilities, and that these will consist of one microphone, at a lectern, on the speakers' table.

5 That the speakers' table will be on the floor of the hall and that the seating will be in a semi-circle around it. You have informed me that this will be done in advance of the meeting.

6 That a lectern will be available.

7 That we will have access to the kitchen in order to provide tea and biscuits after the meeting to those who stay behind to form a supporters' group.

8 That I am representing the organising committee on all matters to do with the hire of the hall and its management on the night, and that you can reach me at any time on the following number: 3525.

I would be grateful for confirmation of this and will be happy to deal with any enquiries from you at any time.

I will be in touch with you 24 hours before the meeting to double-check the details.

Yours faithfully

Bob Trevor

PS The co-ordinator of the meeting and chairperson of our group is Cathy Smith (telephone number 2896) should any problems arise and you are not able to reach me.

if you think that you can get about a hundred people, go for a hall that will seat 80 or 90. It is far better to have people packed in, even with a few having to sit on window-ledges, than a small number in a huge hall suggesting that there really isn't that much support.

My experience is that the chairs in most public halls appear to have been chosen by a sadist. They are nearly always uncomfortable. If there are two or three possible halls and one has more comfortable chairs, take this into account.

If possible, set up your platform at the same level as the audience. The ideal structure for a hall is a semi-circle with the speakers at a table half-surrounded by the audience. A sense of close proximity and community within the meeting is important.

Don't have it over-lit. Obviously the platform must be well lit, but by turning off some of the lights near the back of the hall you create a greater sense of atmosphere.

You may not need a microphone, but if you do for heaven's sake ensure that it is reliable and test it well in advance. I have seen many meetings destroyed by inadequate microphones and speakers disconcerted by members of the audience asking them to speak up.

Your speakers will be much more comfortable if you seat them behind a table where they don't feel totally physically exposed to the audience, and even more comfortable if they are able to speak behind a good solid table lectern. Don't forget to have water available.

Check with your speakers whether they wish to use slides. If they do, it is just as critical to have a reliable projector as it is to have a reliable mike. I myself have been involved in meetings that have been ruined because a slide projector broke down.

Hall organiser's check-list

- Find out all the available halls, and agree with the planning group the most appropriate one, taking into account the size of the audience.
- Visit the hall, talk to its manager, and make sure that you can get in the hall early enough to set it up properly. Discuss all of your requirements for the evening and find out what services are provided in terms of assistance.
- If amplification is required, find out if the hall already has a reliable system and, if not, arrange to get one. Often another organisation involved

or supporting the campaign will have its own.

- Check whether the speakers wish to show film or slides and that the necessary equipment will be available.
- If there are going to be stalls or an exhibition, prepare a layout for the hall so that the audience walks past them/it before going to the seats.
- Check with the hall manager that there is a lectern there. If not, see if you can borrow one from another hall or organisation.
- On the night, be there early enough to have the meeting well set up before anyone arrives. A few flowers and a few posters can make the place look a lot more cheerful and welcoming.
- Check with the caretaker whether there are any regulations about the time meetings must finish. A meeting can be destroyed by the caretaker walking in at a critical moment and announcing that everyone has to leave.
- If the caretaker will not be present on the night, make sure that you have made arrangements about getting entry. I have known an audience to accumulate outside a hall while the organiser is desperately trying to find someone who has the key to let them in.

Publicity manager

There are four main ways you can reach people:

- via local newspapers, radio and television;
- via the communications channels of other organisations;
- via leaflets and posters;
- by word of mouth.

The media

Presumably you will be handling the publicity for the campaign/organisation generally, and therefore will have followed the suggestions we make in our section on publicity (pages 121 to 131). You will therefore have local media contacts, and a local media list.

- As soon as the decisions are taken on the meeting and you have the name of your main speaker, issue a press release to all local media.
- At the same time, write a personal note to contacts, drawing their attention to the press release and asking for maximum publicity.

- Try to get additional news items in the media right up to the date of the meeting.
- If you have a big-name personality coming, arrange for profiles and articles, and then a picture, to appear in local papers.

TV PERSONALITY

DAVID BELLAMY

TO SPEAK AT PROTEST MEETING ON

THREAT TO THE SMITHSVILLE DOWNS

Dr David Bellamy, botanist and well-known television personality, is to speak at a public meeting in Smithsville protesting about plans for a motorway across the Smithsville Downs.

The meeting will be at the town hall on Wednesday, 17 July, and is being organised by the Smithsville Downs Preservation Campaign.

Mrs Cathy Smith, organiser of the campaign, says that concern is now so widespread in the town and surrounding areas that she expects a big turnout.

'We hope to demonstrate to the authorities that local people will not stand by and see this beauty spot destroyed,' she says.

In addition to David Bellamy and Mrs Smith, speakers will be: Grey Jamieson, chairman of the local branch of Friends of the Earth; Warwick Smith, chairman of the Sussex branch of the Council for the Protection of Rural England; and author and popular local personality Ivan Geddis.

Mrs Smith says she has invited representatives of the county council and local MPs to be present.

The meeting, which will be in the Sussex Room of the town hall, will begin at 7.30 pm.

FURTHER INFORMATION: Colin Dennison, Publicity Officer, Smithsville Downs Preservation Campaign, 14 Acacia Avenue, Smithsville. Telephone: Smithsville 3377.

or

Cathy Smith, Co-ordinator of the Campaign.

Telephone: 2896

- If the treasurer will allow you, spend a little bit of money on some small ads in the local newspapers as well.
- Try to hold back some angle until the last week, in order to ensure that you get good publicity on the eve of the meeting.
- Link your meeting publicity up with publicity about the campaign generally, so that people will be reading stories about the cause which with luck will end with a reference to the fact that a public meeting is taking place.

Other organisations

Your campaign will have already been in touch with all other relevant organisations. You should contact their organisers, secretaries and so on to arrange for publicity to all of their members encouraging them to come to the meeting. You should discuss with your planning committee whether it should be a joint meeting with some of these organisations. This will give them an extra incentive to chase up their own members and supporters. The meeting could be 'billed' as 'organised by ... with the support of ... (other organisations)'.

Strenuous efforts to encourage these other organisations to help could have a big pay-off in terms of building up the audience.

Leaflets and posters

Leaflets and posters can often be printed quite cheaply, and they do help.

> ARE YOU AFRAID TO WALK ACROSS SMITHSVILLE FIELDS AT NIGHT?
>
> Why won't the local council answer calls for proper lighting of the paths across the fields, and of nearby streets?
>
> Come to a public meeting to demonstrate your concern and to organise a campaign for action.
>
> Chairperson: well-known author and local celebrity, Paddy Meadowcroft.
>
> St George's Church Hall, near Smithsville Fields, 7.30 pm, Wednesday, 16 September.
>
> Meeting organised by the Smithsville Fields 'Light-Up' Committee.

Obviously, in deciding how you distribute your leaflets, you will want to take into account the areas where people are most affected by the issue. You will need to arrange a leaflet-distributing night if you are going to do it door to door, preferably about five days before the meeting.

Word of mouth

Mention the meeting to family and friends. Encourage people to tell other people. If there are any other events taking place in the area in the preceding weeks, try to get it mentioned by the chairperson at those events, or even arrange with the organisers to put leaflets on the chairs or hand them out at the end of the meeting.

You should aim to create a sense of growing anticipation and excitement about the meeting, a feeling in the local community that if they are not there on the night they could miss something.

There's no magic to it; lots of energy and enthusiasm is the key.

Agenda controller

Your first priority is to get your main personality and you don't want to waste any time, because if your first choice is not available you then have to find someone else. Often busy personalities take some time to reply. Try to make your letter sound as encouraging as possible.

If you haven't received a reply within a week, and you have access to a telephone number, ring him or her. After all, you have waited a week and you are entitled to a reply, even if it is 'No'. Frankly, personalities are busy people, but sometimes they are a little bit inconsiderate of us ordinary mortals as well. You are entitled to know where you stand. You can find this out without being aggressive.

Once you have invited your chairperson and speakers, and got their acceptance, you should then confirm the details in writing.

On the night, you should be present well in advance to greet the speakers, and if possible have arranged a small side-room where they can meet, and perhaps have a glass of wine and relax before the meeting. The publicity officer may well have arranged for local newspaper photographers to come or local radio stations to do a brief interview before the meeting, and this could also be done in that side-room.

Make sure you have arranged with the treasurer that money will be available to cover expenses and so on.

Dear ...

Many thanks for accepting our invitation to speak at/chair the meeting being organised by the Smithsville Downs Preservation Campaign.

I confirm the details: the meeting takes place at 7.30 pm in the Sussex Room at Smithsville Town Hall on Wednesday, 17 July.

We would be grateful if you could be there by 7 pm so that local photographers can have the opportunity to take pictures of the panel, and also in case local radio interviews have been fixed.

I enclose the agenda for the meeting and you will see that we are expecting you to speak for ... minutes.

I also enclose some background details on the Smithsville Downs controversy and the plans for the motorway so that you will know what the issues are and what the up-to-date position is.

Please do not hesitate to advise us of your expenses, and if by any chance you would like a meal before or after the meeting, or overnight accommodation, do please tell me and this can be arranged.

We are now engaged in intensive publicity for the meeting and expect a good turnout.

Everyone looks forward very much to hearing you.

Yours sincerely

Sue Simms

On behalf of Smithsville Downs Preservation Campaign

Dear …

I know from your dedicated campaigning throughout the country/the world that you will be concerned to hear that the beautiful Smithsville Downs are threatened by plans for a motorway.

All concerned with protection of our natural heritage plan to launch a campaign to save them, beginning with a public meeting at 7.30 pm on Wednesday, 17 July, in Smithsville Town Hall, with … and … as the main speakers.

As we are not too far from where you live and I believe you know the downs and will understand our concern, we hope you will be able to spare an evening to take the chair at this meeting.

There is no question that your presence will guarantee its success in terms of drawing a big audience, and your authority and experience will be of considerable help.

We would, incidentally, be happy to organise a bookstall for the sale of your books, and of course will cover your expenses.

I enclose our background notes about the plans for the motorway and about the devastating effect it would have on this beautiful part of the country, and look forward very much to hearing from you, as do all our supporters.

Yours sincerely

Sue Simms

On behalf of Smithsville Downs Preservation Campaign

Treasurer/Chief steward

At the first meeting, discuss with the committee what funds are available. Make a cautious estimate of how much you can obtain from the collection at the meeting. Discuss whether any of the other organisations likely to support you will make a contribution. Fix the likely sum you have available and make this your initial budget.

You can reduce costs considerably if you can get a hall free (some churches and schools will help), if you can get other organisations to loan mikes, projectors and so on, and if you get volunteers to do all the work.

- Put together a budget consisting of the hall hire, cost of hire of any other facilities, publicity, speakers' expenses, catering costs and so on.
- Keep in touch with those with responsibilities to see that they are not going over the top without your being aware of it.
- Get together a team of firm but friendly people who will act as stewards on the night, manning the door and being ready to take up the collection.
- Don't forget to have some collection buckets.
- If you are not making the appeal yourself, take some responsibility for briefing the person who will be.

Other ideas on meetings

Finally on meetings, there are two points worth considering.

First, can you make it more than a public meeting – an event? For instance, in the early days of Shelter, many Shelter groups hired the famous BBC Television film 'Cathy Come Home', and often persuaded the author Jeremy Sandford to speak, as well as myself. As a result they were able to make it a real event – a controversial film with well-known personalities and a wine and cheese party afterwards. This often proved a marvellous foundation for a Shelter group.

Second, if you want the audience to help, don't let them out of the hall until you've got them committed. You don't want to have to chase them up in their own homes if you can avoid it. You have them there, they are interested, they are up to date with the issue, and that is the moment to commit them. There are different ways you can go about this. You can circulate a form for names and addresses and telephone numbers during the meeting. You can get their names and addresses when they arrive or when they leave. But best of all, get them to stay behind and give their names and addresses, thus committing themselves more positively.

Make sure everybody goes away with print material which they can read and think about at home.

And make sure that your follow-up meeting for those who have expressed a desire to be involved takes place quickly. You may think it is worth getting your planning group together the following evening, to review the meeting, and to decide on the next step.

Public speaking

As you will see from the preceding pages, it doesn't take genius to organise a public meeting, just hard work. If you do the work you will have an audience, and you will have an efficient meeting. One thing remains: the speakers must make the right impression.

If you have a major personality, it is important that the personality is well briefed about the issue, and that you have a further word before the meeting to ensure that they are going to be in tune with the theme of the meeting.

But what about you, the organiser, who will have to speak on behalf of your own campaign?

Outline of speech by Mrs Cathy Smith at public meeting organised by the Smithsville Downs Preservation Campaign

1. Plans for the motorway. Who decides and what their proposals are. What the timescale is.
2. Where the motorway will go. The damage it will do to Smithsville Downs.
3. Why we should care: environmental protection for future generations, save recreational facilities today, halt damage to the town as a recreational attraction etc.
4. Why a campaign has been set up.
5. The other organisations and people who support it.
6. What we must do now to persuade the authorities to change their minds.
7. How you can help.

You may say: 'I am not a speaker.' Well, no one is ... to begin with. There is, in fact, not much to it, provided you follow a few basic rules, the first being not to exaggerate the difficulties in your own mind. Don't forget that this audience has come because they're interested and most of them are supportive. They want to hear what you have to say and they want to be sympathetic. All you need do is talk directly, factually, sincerely and relatively briefly.

- Prepare an outline of your speech and then list under the different headings the key points you wish to make.
- Make your key points and only your key points. Don't go on too long; 99.999 per cent of speakers do that. If you are different, they'll love you for that alone.
- Don't be too emotional. Try and keep to the facts and let your argument speak for itself. People get embarrassed if a speaker is excessively emotional.
- Don't be too aggressive. The audience will suspect you if you are. They will be impressed if you appear good humoured, reasonable, direct and yet at the same time concerned. This is probably what you are like anyway; don't pretend to be someone different.
- You don't have to shout or rant. Speak to the audience as you might to someone in your own home, directly, to the point, and assuming them to be sympathetic. They'll love you. Honestly.

CHASING THE MONEY

Groan!

That's what I said. GROAN. Let's be honest, fund-raising is the hardest part of campaigning. Raising money is the eternal problem.

Nevertheless, it has to be done. That being the case, the following suggestions may help.

How to plan fund-raising

Appoint a treasurer/fund-raiser who will be the member of your group responsible for both raising and looking after the money. (Looking after the money is a responsible task: it should be properly banked, all donations should be receipted, and proper accounts should be produced. Your opponents would just love to raise a question mark over your whole campaign by suggesting dishonesty or financial irresponsibility.)

Smithsville Housing Action Committee

CAMPAIGN TO STOP CIVIC CENTRE

INCOME AND EXPENDITURE BUDGET

Money required	£
Photocopying of documents, reports, plans etc	50.00
Production of substantial report on civic centre proposal, on the capacity of town hall to cope as it is, and other uses for money, and circulation of the report to councillors, MPs, media etc	260.00
Production of mass leaflet summarising report	240.00
Public meeting	100.00
Correspondence to MPs, authorities	50.00
Other campaigning expenses	300.00
TOTAL REQUIRED	1000.00

Fund-raising activity	
Personal donations by members of SHACs committee (20 members × £5)	100.00
Donations by substantial local organisations supportive of the cause (6 organisations × £50)	300.00
Public meeting collection	50.00
Charge for additional copies of the report to organisations etc	50.00
Appeal letter	200.00
Jumble sale	150.00
Work day	150.00
TOTAL	1000.00

TIMETABLE OF MONEY REQUIRED

At beginning:	£100
After 2 months:	£400
Within 9 months:	£500

Estimate how much money you will need – you need a realistic fund-raising target. *Work out when you will need it.* It can be frightening to be faced with a substantial fund-raising target with the implication that the money is all needed at once. If, in fact, it is needed over a year, then your fund-raising can be organised in such a way that you have plenty of time to do it, and the money is raised when it is needed.

Having achieved a realistic budget, *break the fund-raising target down into manageable sums.* It can look a lot less imposing in this way. Those manageable sums could be made up of the different fund-raising ideas which follow.

Ways of fund-raising

Don't expect others to give if you don't care enough to give yourself. The first source of income must be you. You care about it more than almost anyone else, otherwise you would not be organising the campaign. At your first meeting, try to get all of the members to put some money down on the spot so that you have an immediate initial sum.

You are already making contact with all *other organisations* in the area which may be sympathetic to your cause. One of the first things you should do is ask them to contribute to the finances. Tell them what your fund-raising requirements are and don't be afraid to tell them exactly how much you would like them to contribute.

It's always marvellous if you can cover part of your budget by *one substantial donation.* Is there a wealthy person, organisation or even company in the area that is sympathetic to your cause and would be likely to write a cheque for a substantial sum? Check whether you have anyone involved in the campaign who knows such a person personally, for this is the approach most likely to succeed. If you don't, you have a choice between seeking an appointment, at which you explain why they should donate, or writing an appeal letter.

Choose as your fund-raising target the *people most likely to be affected.* If, for instance, you are raising money for a campaign to have pedestrian facilities for children at a particular school improved, it makes sense to begin by appealing to the parents of those children.

Are there any *charities or trusts known to support worthy causes* in your area that may find your campaign attractive? Find out what their objectives are, and whether an appeal letter to them is likely to have a sympathetic response. Try to get a list of the trustees to see if you know anybody on it, not so much for special pleading as to be briefed by them on the likelihood

An appeal letter by Brian Hunter, secretary of the Smithsville Housing Action Committee, to a wealthy local resident

Dear ...

In the past you have made a number of generous donations to our work to help homeless families in this area.

We know, too, from a letter that you wrote to the Smithsville Standard some weeks back, that you are a critic of wasteful expenditure by the local council.

We believe, therefore, that you will be concerned to hear that the council plans to build a modern civic centre costing some £20 million.

My fellow members of SHAC, and others concerned with the many practical and urgent needs of the town, believe that there will be widespread public opposition to this plan and that it can be stopped.

We know we can demonstrate that the existing town hall, and other facilities of the town, are adequate, and we are in the process of producing a detailed report to demonstrate this. But to pay for the widespread circulation of our report, and for a campaign of public education on the matter, we need money and we hope very much you will consider being generous once more and will make a contribution.

We need at least £1,000. Of course, we do not look to you for such a substantial sum, but if you could get us started with a donation, it would be enormously encouraging to all involved. We would be only too pleased to come and see you and discuss the matter further if that would be useful.

With very best wishes and thanks once more for your past support.

Yours sincerely

Brian Hunter

LETTER TO THE SUSSEX RURAL PRESERVATION TRUST

From Cathy Smith

Dear Secretary

The people of Smithsville have been grateful for the grants your trust has made over the years to organisations trying to protect our natural heritage, the beautiful countryside of this area.

We believe your trust will be concerned to hear that there are plans for a motorway which would virtually destroy our Smithsville Downs.

Many individuals and organisations concerned to protect the downs, which combine their beauty with many practical recreational advantages for the people of Smithsville and the surrounding area, have formed an organisation to oppose the building of this motorway. But it may turn out to be expensive. Not only do we have to pay for research into alternative paths for the motorway and organise a public education campaign, but we may need to take part in a public inquiry.

We have set ourselves an initial fund-raising target of £10,000, but may need more.

We hope very much that your trust will consider our urgent need and make a substantial contribution, which will be of enormous encouragement to all involved. In itself it will also be an indication to the authorities that our cause should be taken seriously.

I enclose a list of our committee and its supporters, our objectives, our campaign plan and some local news clippings. I also enclose some photographs of the area and a brief history of it. We would be happy to make available any more information you might require.

We look forward to hearing from you.

Yours sincerely

Cathy Smith

Co-ordinator, Smithsville Downs Preservation Campaign

of your appeal achieving success. Alternatively, ring up the secretary and ask if they would be good enough to tell you whether your cause is likely to be relevant to that trust.

If you are not in conflict with *the local council*, or if you are campaigning for a cause that the council is sympathetic to, write a formal letter of appeal for help to the chief executive. It will definitely go before the relevant committee and you may be pleasantly surprised and receive a grant.

Don't forget to *link your fund-raising needs to all you do.* If you organise a meeting, take a collection. If you are organising any other kind of event, or speaking at a meeting of any other organisation, mention the need for money. If you are having a publicity stall in the local market or the High Street to promote the cause, have a collection bucket as well.

Consider *a fund-raising event*. There are two kinds:

- *Events you organise for yourselves*. For instance, if you are planning to have a committee meeting, why not arrange for it to be followed by a wine and cheese party? Your committee could meet at 7.30 pm, and at 9.00 pm be joined by friends, husbands, wives and so on for a wine and cheese party to which everyone contributes. You spend money on recreation anyway; why not think of things that you might do together that can benefit the cause?
- *Events for others*. Don't be afraid of the tried and tested regulars – jumble sales, Christmas toy fairs, summer fetes, and the like. The reason they recur and recur is because they actually work. These have to be organised with the same detail that you have to apply to organising a public meeting. You should have a special meeting to plan the event, assign tasks to different members of the committee, and approach it with the same attention to detail.

Try to *get young people involved*. If a local youth group or school will organise a fund-raising activity, you'll be surprised at how effective they can be and also how they end up by involving their parents as well.

What about work days? Members of the group and supporters let it be known that they are available as a workforce on a selected number of days – usually Saturdays – during the year in return for a fixed donation to the cause. Somebody who has a relatively small piece of wasteland to be cleared, or a local business that needs additional help at certain times of the year, will often be pleased to be offered a cheerful, enthusiastic workforce at what are probably competitive rates.

Consider getting your supporters together for *a collection* – door to door, or a street collection or a pub collection. Check with the local police about the licence you require – and organise it well, so that your collectors aren't duplicating effort. If you organise a collection, it is important that your collectors are well briefed on the issue and friendly and courteous. This is a good way of promoting the cause generally, so even where you don't get a donation, you should leave a leaflet. It often makes sense also to ask people to sign a petition. It is worth considering not beginning your doorstep conversation with an appeal for funds, but actually asking the person on the doorstep first if they support your cause and whether they will sign a petition. If they say 'Yes', then ask them if they would also make a donation.

General points about fund-raising

- There is no such thing as a fund-raising machine. Fund-raising has to be done by people. The treasurer/fund-raiser should try to create a special subcommittee to help and they in turn should seek to recruit as many helpers as possible.
- Given that I began this section by saying that fund-raising was a 'groan', try to combat this by making it fun. The more you can make fund-raising enjoyable, and come up with events and activities that everybody enjoys, the less of a problem it will be seen to be.
- The more effective your campaign, the easier it will be to raise money. And a high profile, plenty of publicity and signs that you are winning will all help. Try to link your fund-raising to other activities of the campaign so that one can feed on the other.
- Don't overlook the fact that you can reduce your financial needs by persuading people to donate time or facilities for free. Try to incorporate in your group people with professional skills and to persuade local tradesmen, printers and so on to help out for the sake of the cause. Lean on the other organisations who are supporting you for any services they can offer. They may have duplicating machines, photocopiers or small printing machines, microphones and projectors, and even equipment for funfairs.

All that said, fund-raising, particularly some of the laws associated with various ways of doing it, calls for a lot of detailed professional advice that we ourselves are not equipped to offer.

Print and Publicity

See also page 107.

Once you have decided that you are running a public campaign, publicity becomes the name of the game.

The first step is to appoint a print and publicity officer, who will be responsible for publicising your activities via the media, publicity events and the production of print material. This section is directed almost entirely to that essential member of the campaign team.

What qualities do you require? Ideally (although not essentially) some professional qualification. If you work in the media, or in the advertising or public relations business, so much the better. But, above all, publicity – like every other aspect of campaigning – calls for the three Es – enthusiasm, energy and enterprise.

- *Enthusiasm,* because enthusiasm is infectious.
- *Energy,* because there is a lot of hard work involved.
- *Enterprise,* because a publicity officer must not only do the obvious but be quick to seize opportunities and be able to come up with original ideas.

Let's assume you have not worked in the media or publicity business before. In this case, before you even begin publicising your campaign, there are two essential steps you will have to take: investigate your local media and organise a publicity plan.

Getting to know your local media

- Write out a list of every newspaper or magazine covering your area, together with local radio stations and any local television programme.
- Find out all you can about them. How do they treat news? What is their style? When do they go to press? Who are the reporters or feature writers who seem interested in issues like yours?
- Put together a media profile consisting of:
  a) name of publication or programme,

  b) name of news editor,

  c) name of sympathetic journalists,

  d) deadline,

  e) any other useful information about them.

Putting together a publicity plan

Remember that you will not want to use all your good ideas at once. Assuming that you expect the campaign to run for some time, you should plan it so that you don't run out of publicity ideas in the first week or two.

At the same time, your aim should be to create the impression of momentum building behind the campaign.

Publicity plan

A step-by-step programme could be as follows:

- Make contact with key individuals in the media who are likely to be sympathetic, to tip them off that a campaign is planned and seek their advice as to how it could best be covered by their newspaper or programme.
- Send an official press release announcing that a campaign is being launched, who is organising it and what the first event is likely to be.
- One week before the public meeting, hold a press conference, or alternatively issue a major press release containing the result of your advance work or research, initial personalities and the campaign's objectives. Announce your public meeting or opening event.
- Issue a formal invitation to local media to attend the public meeting and check by telephone that they are going to come.
- If you have a leading personality speaking at the meeting, try to arrange a pre-meeting interview or profile to build up interest.
- If some of the media do not turn up on the night, prepare a brief press release of the event overnight and deliver it to the appropriate addresses early the next day.
- As soon as possible after the public meeting issue a press release saying what the campaign intends to do next.

Press releases

- Keep them brief.
- Keep them to the point.
- Write them in newspaper style.
- Always begin with the famous five Ws – what, who, where, when and why. If you answer these questions, it is unlikely that you will have missed any key ingredients from your press release.
- Keep them factual and as credible as possible.

Often a newspaper will run the press release as written if you follow newspaper style, and therefore it is worth presenting it in an acceptable way:

SMITHSVILLE DOWNS PRESERVATION CAMPAIGN

Publicity Officer Colin Dennison – 14 Acacia Avenue, Smithsville. Telephone: Smithsville 3377

Major campaign to be launched to save Smithsville Downs
A major campaign, involving several Smithsville organisations and well-known personalities, is to be launched to save the Smithsville Downs, currently threatened by plans for a motorway.

Organisations with representatives on the steering committee include the Smithsville branch of the Council for the Protection of Rural England, Friends of the Earth, the Conservation Society, and 'Save Britain's Heritage'.

The co-ordinator of the campaign, Cathy Smith, who has published a book of her paintings of the Smithsville Downs, says that she believes it will attract 'overwhelming support throughout the area'.

Mrs Smith said that the steering committee was planning a public meeting for 17 July in the town hall to launch the campaign. It was hoped that Dr David Bellamy would be speaking.

The new motorway is intended to help Londoners and others reach the south-coast resorts more quickly. Plans published by the Ministry of Transport suggest that it will cut across the Smithsville Downs, popular for picnics and walks at the weekends, and one of the most beautiful parts of the Sussex countryside.

The steering committee hopes to be able to demonstrate that there is an alternative route for such a motorway which would be less damaging to the countryside.

The steering committee hopes to present detailed recommendations, together with a petition, to the Ministry of Transport, and to seek the support of the borough and county councils. 'Obviously we hope they will see reason,' Mrs Smith comments. 'We can assure the ministry that if it does not, the people of this area will not stand by and see the downs demolished without a fight.'

Further information: Colin Dennison, Publicity Officer, Smithsville 3377

OR

Cathy Smith, Smithsville 2896

typed in double spacing, with plenty of space between paragraphs and in the margins. Don't forget to put a contact name and telephone number at the end. If you have any picture ideas, send a copy to the picture editor with a letter suggesting what the photograph could be.

Personal contacts

The ideal for any campaign is to have a reporter on each local newspaper who is personally interested in the cause and with whom you can keep in regular contact. This saves having to educate each new reporter and means that the reporter will often act as an agent within the newspaper, promoting the idea. Make a point of establishing friendly relations with such contacts, but not becoming a bore; only contact them when you have something to say or when you want to ask advice.

To the Editor

The Smithsville Standard

Sir,

Press Conference to launch the
Smithsville Downs Preservation Campaign

The press conference to launch this major campaign will take place at 11.00 am on Thursday, 23 July, and we hope you will be represented.

In addition to the representatives of the campaign, the press conference will be addressed by councillors from both the borough and county councils, and by representatives of other local organisations.

We will be publishing at the press conference our own alternative proposal for the motorway to the south coast, and illustrations of the likely damage to the downs were the present plans to proceed.

Further information can be obtained from:

Colin Dennison

Smithsville 3377

Press conference

You are only likely to have a press conference if you really have a substantial story and if there are several media outlets in the area. If there are only a couple of newspapers, it is better to see them separately.

The advantage of a press conference is that it is an event in its own right, and still sufficiently unusual at local level to arouse the curiosity of the media. But it must be justified – journalists won't waste time attending a bad press conference by the same campaign twice.

Other sections of your local newspaper

Don't forget that the news pages are only part of a newspaper.

The letters to the editor page offers plenty of opportunities to make short, sharp points, and often to get several people writing in on different angles of the same issue. A controversy can really build up via this page.

Don't forget the women's page; many campaigns are of special interest to women and the women's editor is often pleased to have ideas for her regular page or column.

Some newspapers have a features editor who has to come up with longer, in-depth articles and is also constantly looking for new ideas.

An enterprising pictures editor is always pleased to hear from members of the public who can propose a good photograph.

National newspapers

A local campaign can often get a big 'lift' by making the national newspapers.

Check if there is a news agency in your area which feeds the national newspapers with stories. It will be constantly looking for opportunities to sell ideas to the 'nationals' because this is how it makes its living. If there is a local news agency, visit it and see whether there is any national potential in what you are doing.

Alternatively, try a letter to *The Times* or another national newspaper. The publication in the letters to the editor page of a national newspaper of a small item about a local campaign with some national significance can lead to national radio or television interest.

A brief letter like the sample included here tries to achieve national publicity for a local cause, and at the same time alerts the national media to a campaign that just might capture their interest.

LETTER TO THE TIMES

From Cathy Smith

Sir

You quote the Minister of Transport (Times 7 July) as saying that 'It should be possible to cater for the needs of the motorist without destroying our natural heritage.'

Perhaps he is unaware of the ministry's plans to build a motorway across 'the Smithsville Downs', not only a treasured recreational facility for this area, but one of the most beautiful pieces of parkland in the country.

He may like to know that a major campaign is planned to save the downs, with the support of the local borough and county councils, both currently ruled by members of his own party. If he really means what he says, the people of this area – and we believe others throughout the country who really care about our natural heritage – will look for a quick response from him and a ministerial change of plan.

Yours faithfully

Cathy Smith

Responding to events

Often you will be telephoned by the local newspaper and asked to comment on something the authorities have done, or something your opponents have said.

React calmly, and make sure that your comment is both comprehensive and to the point. Don't launch a violent attack which makes your response sound hysterical. Often you can demolish an opponent in one paragraph by a calm, factual reply:

> I note the chairperson of the planning committee says that the proposed junction will not constitute a hazard; perhaps he could explain why an exactly similar junction 400 yards away on the other side of the town square has the highest accident figures for anywhere in the country.

Such a response can demolish the case made by the chairperson of planning, and leave a big question mark in the mind of the reader.

Involving other people

Although you are responsible for publicity, that doesn't mean you shouldn't involve other people.

People make news; the more you can get others writing to the newspapers or organising their own publicity events, linked up with what you are doing, the better.

Finally, don't be inhibited by the media. There is no mystery about the media; they are made up of quite ordinary people, all employed to collect and publish regularly huge quantities of news and features. They are hungry for ideas, and often more than willing to help. If you approach them in a businesslike but friendly way, try to understand their problems and present your stories in a way that is helpful to them, you will be surprised at how effective a publicist you can be. And don't forget that local journalists are usually members of your community. If you are having social events or parties, invite them along. Involve them in your business just as you are involving yourself in theirs.

Presenting your case in print

See also N for Newspaper, pages 62 to 64.

When it comes to putting your case on paper, or in print, the aims must be:

- *say what you want to say*

  and

- *create the impression you want to create*

in the form most acceptable to those who you wish to reach within the probably limited budget you have. It is not money that decides whether your print material is effective (although money always helps), but its clarity and style.

Try to incorporate in your group a graphic designer, or even a design student, who can create an image for your campaign, perhaps a logo or symbol, and a common 'look' for all your material.

Given that all print material costs some money, it clearly makes sense to produce only what you really need, and not to rush off producing leaflets, posters, car stickers and so on without a reason.

If you are going to produce a leaflet, who is it for? How many will you need? What is it you want to say? How are you going to be able to distribute it?

Leaflets

These will normally be to advertise a meeting or some other event, to make people more aware of the issues generally, or to appeal for specific help.

They should be attractive, have a sense of immediacy and use a minimum number of words.

Posters

These will normally be to advertise an event, or to convey a simple dramatic message. (For instance, I once lived in a street threatened by plans for a diversion of heavy traffic. Throughout the area we put up a poster with a photograph of the street being broken into two and the simple slogan 'Traffic is destroying Leighton Road'.)

Newspapers or news-sheets

If your campaign is likely to run for some time, then one way of keeping people up to date and developing a sense of momentum is to produce a regular news-sheet. This will not just be an updater, but will also advertise any activities you plan and appeal for help.

Newspapers offer a flexible format and, because they represent the way most people are accustomed to assimilating information, tend to be read. Liberal Party activists throughout Britain have made a major impact with the widespread distribution of their local *Focus* newsletters.

Reports

Sometimes you will wish to publish the research behind your campaign together with alternative proposals in the form of a report. This can often be done by the use of a photocopier or a duplicating machine, but an inexpensive card-cover can be printed in order that it has an appearance of substance.

Using print in the campaign

It is a good idea to have one individual responsible for the production of the campaign's print material, but decisions about what should be produced and when should be taken by the entire group.

Let's say you are organising a campaign likely to run for a year or two. You may decide on the following:

1 A quarterly 4-page newspaper, probably produced by someone with an offset litho machine (you may find another voluntary group in the area which has one, or you may have to make it an arrangement with a cheap, and hopefully supportive, local printer). It will report on how the campaign is developing and on the issue generally, and also advertise planned activities. The newspaper will not be timed to be exactly quarterly, but instead linked to major campaign events or to crucial decision-making meetings by the local authority or whatever.

2 A 2-page leaflet for widespread dissemination, stating as briefly as possible a) what the issue is, b) that a campaign has been created and c) how people can get in touch and why they should help.

3 A dramatic small poster for extensive display in the area most affected by the issue and most likely to respond to the campaign.

Try to create a common image that will be perpetuated throughout the campaign, so that people only have to see a symbol or a leaflet from your campaign to know what it is about.

This is where a designer will be helpful. If you don't have a designer in your group, you may be able to persuade a local art college or even a senior art class at a local school to have a go at designing your material. It would be good practical experience for them, and the results would probably be a lot better than you would manage yourself.

Keep the copy in all your material brief. Say only what you need to say to capture interest and attention. This is particularly important for the leaflets. Try to achieve a sense of urgency with the design and keep the wording as factual as possible. People will not respond positively to material they believe to be hysterical, or that gives them the impression that there's some kind of personality battle going on.

Try to communicate in your print material the breadth of support you have, indicating (if you can) that it's non-party political and has the support of other organisations.

And remember: before you finalise your plan to print a leaflet or news-sheet, ask yourself whom you are trying to reach and what you want to say to them. Do not make the mistake of many campaigners, of producing a leaflet that is self-indulgent in the sense that it is really speaking to themselves rather than reaching out to its audience.

Checklist for your print organiser

- Establish with the group why they want the leaflet produced and who it is for.
- Establish the number required.
- Find someone who will design it for nothing.
- Try to find an organisation that can print it free of charge, except for the cost of paper, or otherwise try to find a friendly printer who will do it as cheaply as possible.
- Establish with the group when it has to be produced.
- Avoid a group discussion about the copy (10 or 15 people can't write a leaflet) but do consult the group co-ordinator, the group publicist and any others whom you think might make a special input.
- When the leaflet is designed and written, check the facts with the utmost care.
- Also check that the leaflet *does* a) tell people exactly what the issue is; b) tell people exactly what your campaign is; c) tell people how they can contact you. In other words, make sure the leaflet does the job it is supposed to do.
- Check that there are no remarks in the leaflet that could be libellous. Work on the principle 'If in doubt, leave it out.' Hopefully there will be a solicitor or even a journalist on your committee who can advise from a knowledge of the law of libel.
- Arrange to see a proof, or an early copy of the leaflet, before they are all printed in order to do a final check, and get someone else to look at it as well. It is amazing how you can look and look at a leaflet and be convinced that it is right, and yet there can still be an error somewhere. Remember: if these are printing errors or obvious mistakes the public will lose confidence in the authority of the group.
- Check that the leaflet has an imprint. The printer's and the publisher's name and address must be on all publications.
- Finally, don't forget the old maxim that 'a picture is worth a thousand words,' and don't be afraid to use drawings, photographs or cartoons to make your point.

4 Lobbying

Leighton Andrews

It is everyone's right to approach their elected representatives on a matter of personal or political concern. In a volatile political climate particularly, most MPs and councillors are prepared to listen and will respond to a well-argued case.

They can be your best allies, but remember that there are real limits to what even they can do.

As always, it is necessary to begin with the key questions:

- Who will make the decision?
- How much time is there to influence the decision?
- What is the most effective way to lobby the decision-takers and how can your MP or councillors help you do this?

Consider, for example, the hypothetical Smithsville campaigns. For Cathy Smith, trying to stop the motorway, the answers to these three questions will be:

1 The government, through the Department of Transport (probably with some input from the Department of the Environment); and the local council.

2 There's a reasonable period of time for a campaign. Motorways can take years to build and are subject to variations in public expenditure, and planning consultations may contribute to delays.

3 The support of the two MPs and the two councils is crucial.

Brian Hunter knows precisely who is responsible for the decision he wants to affect. The borough council will decide on its own civic centre, probably at a full council meeting. There is no real role for government, but local MPs may help to apply pressure.

Augustine Kirkwood knows that the government is responsible for the decision to cut housing benefit to pensioners. She has to act quickly and the local MPs are her only points of access to government.

Marie Sheedy knows it's the council's responsibility to repair the lighting. It shouldn't need any sort of political decision to get it fixed – she just needs the officers to act, but pressure from councillors could be necessary.

How then do they make their contacts and lobby these decision-takers effectively?

Finding out about your MP

There are a number of things you need to know before approaching your MP. First, if you're concerned about a specifically local matter, which constituency does it actually affect? Second, what are the MP's politics, and is his or her party in government or in opposition? Third, does your MP have a direct interest in the subject?

The support you are likely to get from your MP depends on whether he or she is a member of the governing party or the opposition. There are generally three possible scenarios where your MP might support you:

1 Your MP is a member of the governing party and there is no clear ideological or policy reason why the MP or the party should oppose you. This is the most favourable scenario and one in which your MP may be able to help you win your case swiftly. They can talk directly to ministers, their parliamentary private secretaries and government whips, and have more chance of a sympathetic hearing than do opposition MPs.

2 Your MP is a member of the governing party and is prepared to back your case even though it is against the expressed policy of the party. Thus he or she may vote against the party whip. This MP could be a great help to your campaign. He or she will become a focus for press and media attention locally and indeed nationally if the issue is sufficiently topical or controversial.

3 Your MP is an opposition member prepared to fight your case against the government through all the means available, and ready to enlist the help of the party in the House of Commons.

Now to the MP's interest. In a strict parliamentary sense, this refers to business, sponsorship, consultancies and other pecuniary interests recorded in the Register of Members' Interests annually. But MPs often have special policy interests as well.

As politics becomes more specialised, MPs often try to become expert in one or two fields of policy. It may be that they hope to become ministers in that area; it may reflect their interests before they went into politics full-time. Ambitious MPs will probably develop a variety of interests.

MPs can follow their political interests in a variety of ways.

There are the official committees of the House of Commons intended to shadow or examine the work of a particular government department. These are known as *select committees*, and are made up of MPs drawn from the back benches, generally weighted slightly in favour of the governing party. So you have the transport select committee, the environment select committee and so on. Next there are the parliamentary Labour and Conservative Parties' *back-bench committees* on a wide range of subjects. Sometimes these are more specific than the select committees. The party back-bench committees may hold regular meetings with their front-bench or opposition spokespeople. They appoint their own officers from back-benchers considered expert in their subjects, who may or may not be members of the relevant select committee.

Then there are *all-party groups*, ranging in their interests from cycling to penal reform. There are reckoned to be nearly a hundred of these listed at any one time, though some meet more frequently than others. Some exist only on paper. Some may be concerned with the problems of a particular country, acting as a kind of friendship group. Very often all-party groups have informal links with national campaigns, charities or pressure groups of one kind or another. There is also a variety of trade union groups amongst the Labour Party MPs.

Your MP may be an active member, even an officer, of one of these committees. There are a number of ways to find this out.

Your reference library will contain one of a number of useful works of reference which give biographies and details of members' interests in particular subjects: *The Times Guide to the House of Commons* (published after each general election); *Dods* (updated annually, this also gives information on members of the House of Lords); and *Who's Who*.

A simpler guide is *Vachers* (updated quarterly), which lists the key select committees and back-bench committees (*not* all-party groups) and their members.

The Public Information Office at the House of Commons (071-219 4272) answers a variety of queries, including requests for information on all-party groups. On occasion they may be able to help with enquiries on which subjects MPs have spoken or asked questions on. These are now stored on computer on the Parliamentary On-Line Information Service (POLIS).

The Journal and Information Office (071-219 3107) handles enquiries for the House of Lords.

If you are going to be running a campaign over a long period of time it may be worth trying to keep a record of activities or comments made by your MP on the subject with which you are concerned. The campaign publicity officer, if you have one, should be able to monitor any local or national press coverage of speeches made by your MP. You may also want to consult the indexes of Hansard, which your reference library may have. If you are a branch of a national campaign, your central organisation may have information on your MP's activities.

How to reach your MP

Most MPs hold a surgery in their constituencies either weekly or monthly. It may be in one central place each time or it may rotate between the council wards, possibly being held in a school, a library or at the party offices. In more rural areas, surgeries tend to rotate between villages. Surgeries are generally held on Saturday mornings or Friday evenings. They tend to be advertised in local papers or local libraries. The local party offices can tell you where they are.

MPs tend to be in Westminster between Monday lunchtime and late Thursday evening/early Friday morning. They can be telephoned direct at the House of Commons (main switchboard number 071-219 3000). Hours of official business in the chamber of the House of Commons are roughly 2.30–10.30 pm Monday–Thursday (though frequently later) and 9.30–3.30 pm on Fridays. There are committee meetings both morning and afternoon from Tuesday to Thursday and sometimes in the evening. Usually the best time to get them on the telephone is before noon.

Most MPs employ a secretary – either based at the House of Commons or, occasionally, in the constituency – who will deal with appointments and correspondence. Some employ a researcher, who if sympathetic is well worth cultivating.

MPs can be visited at the House of Commons but it is best to arrange an appointment beforehand. Those without appointments follow the 'green card' procedure: in the central lobby of the House of Commons they fill in a green appointment card offered by the policeman on duty, and this is then conveyed to the member if he or she is in the building. This can take some time.

Parliament tends to be in recess from the end of July to the middle of October. The new 'session' begins in November with the Queen's speech.

Christmas recess tends to last about three weeks, Easter two weeks and Whitsun one week.

Involving your MP

Most MPs will have their own sense of what is politically important, and their own interests and their own prejudices against certain kinds of groups. Every day their postbags will be full of mail from a colourful array of organisations. And every day a large amount of mail is immediately tossed away, possibly by MPs' secretaries. This is unlikely, however, with a constituency letter, especially if it is well written.

Here are a few useful rules for contact with MPs:

- If you can, always write. This establishes your credentials and means you don't have to go through a long rigmarole with a secretary on the telephone explaining who you are and what the issue is. Write even if you want to see your MP at the surgery. This allows MPs to brief themselves on the issue and on your organisation.
- If you've met the MP before, make the most of the fact. Start your letter with the words 'You may recall we met (when you came to speak to my church group for a meeting on drug abuse, which I chaired)'. MPs feel they ought to remember people who've been active in some local committee. Of course, if the last time you met your MP you poured soup into his or her lap or declared that you wouldn't vote for him or her if there was no one else on the ballot paper, you may not want to start the letter in this way. Indeed you probably aren't the right person to be writing the letter in the first place.
- Since you are involved in a local campaign and thus hard to ignore, make sure this is plainly stated in the letter as well as the letterhead.
- If you know your MP has a deep and long-standing interest in the subject on which you are writing, it helps to mention in your first paragraph a recent speech or question he or she has made or asked.
- If it is a national issue but there is a special constituency reason why your MP should be concerned about it, mention this.

SMITHSVILLE PENSIONERS ACTION GROUP

10 Town Street
Smithsville

Sir Anthony Jones Esq MP
House of Commons
London SW1A 0AA

Dear Sir Anthony

RE: Housing Benefit changes

You may remember that we met last year when you spoke to the AGM of the Smithsville Pensioners Action Group on 'the Prospect for Pensioners'. I was delighted to see your recent speech on the impact of inflation on the pensioner, in which you kindly referred to the study we have carried out here.

I am writing to you now about the recent announcement that there will be a reduction in housing benefit for pensioners. I understand that the government is unlikely to introduce its proposals for two months, so there is still time to influence their decision.

As you know, in Smithsville 23 per cent of our population is retired – quite a high figure. Of these 23,000 people, I believe 11,500 will lose money under the new regulations. For some the reductions could run into several pounds a week. These figures are based on calculations from government answers in Hansard which show that half of all pensioners will be affected. Pensioners in Smithsville are very disturbed at these plans. I know many have been in touch with you in the last year over the problems they have making ends meet.

I wonder if you will be prepared to join us in opposing these proposals, by writing to the minister responsible, and by signing the Early Day Motion No 100 which I understand refers to this issue.

I attach more detailed information on the government's proposals. I will of course be very happy to supply any further information you may require.

Yours sincerely

Augustine Kirkwood

Secretary

- Keep the letter as short as possible. Try to get the basic point over in the first few paragraphs and expand on it in subsequent paragraphs, as with a press release. Try to keep your comments to one side of paper, or two at most.
- Unless you know your MP well enough to write a personal handwritten letter, type your letter. MPs hate ploughing through handwritten letters.
- Never send your MP a duplicated letter passed on by national headquarters with just the MP's name and your signature to fill in. Never print duplicated letters for your members to send in. These impress no one. If an issue is important, it is important enough to write personal letters about. Duplicated handout letters are the first to be junked.
- Always attune your letter to each MP you are writing to.
- If you know someone who has a closer contact with your MP than you do, either get them to write on your behalf, if appropriate, or get them to write supporting your case and saying they are sure the MP will soon be hearing from you.

Keeping your MP informed

An established local pressure group or charity should maintain contacts with local MPs on a regular basis.

Involving MPs in your main events (eg speaking at your annual general meeting or opening some new facility you have organised) will make them readier to respond when you urgently need help. Of course, you should not try to overdo this: MPs' diaries are very full at any time, particularly those belonging to MPs whose constituencies are far from London who have to cram all constituency engagements into weekends and the recess. But it should be part of your normal public relations activity to ensure that your MP knows that you are a worthwhile and active local organisation. He or she will be keener to attend your events if it is clear that you are organising publicity that may result in local press photos.

In any case, you should keep your MP on your mailing list for useful pieces of information. These may not be read at the time they are received, but they are likely to be kept on file. MPs need to know who to go to as much as anyone else; on occasions they may be able to use your material as background for speeches.

This section concentrates on involving your MP and what he or she can do for you at Westminster. Remember, however, that your MP, being a public figure in your locality, can add considerably to your publicity value if he or she supports your case. Try to find a specific event in which you can involve him or her, and ensure that the local press, television and radio are informed and come along and record the event.

As with other public figures, you can get MPs to:

- lend their names to an appeal for money, volunteers or materials;
- speak at meetings on your behalf;
- make statements in support of the policy aims which you are trying to achieve;
- use influence with the local council or other groups in the locality.

Arranging to meet your MP

You do not need a meeting with your MP at every stage of your campaign. If a degree of sympathy exists and you can suggest specific actions to your MP in a simple letter, it is far better to do that: it is less effort for both sides. But there are occasions when meetings are essential and avoid delays, particularly when you think your MP may want to question you further.

You may need a meeting with your MP if the case is complex and your argument cannot be conveyed in a simple letter – particularly if you have a well-organised opposition whose arguments need countering. Also you may be at a loss about what to do next, and think your MP will be better able to focus on the correct channels of influence.

To arrange a meeting, write, then follow up your letter after one or two days with a telephone call to the MP's secretary. Be aware that if you turn up unannounced at an MP's surgery, you are quite likely to get only a few minutes. So make clear in your letter how much time you think you will need and why. If you want a meeting and aren't sure of your MP's view, remember it is important to demonstrate great public concern on the issue and support for your case.

SMITHSVILLE DOWNS PRESERVATION CAMPAIGN

Sir Anthony Jones MP
House of Commons
London SW1A 0AA

Dear Sir Anthony

Re: Proposed motorway link across Smithsville Downs

You will be aware of the latest plan from the Department of Transport that the new motorway link to the south coast should cut across the Smithsville Downs, one of the most important local sites of natural beauty.

While there is a need for an improvement to our transport system to reduce the flow of traffic into the centre of Smithsville, this new motorway link is not the answer. You will no doubt have seen the excellent leading article on this subject in the Smithsville Standard this week, which concluded that the motorway link should be built elsewhere (copy enclosed).

I have been associated with the promotion of the downs, one of our greatest tourist attractions, over many years. My paintings of the downs are frequently bought by visitors to the area as souvenirs.

I believe that the motorway plans will be catastrophic for the downs. Not only will they be particularly damaging to a beautiful area and to the wildlife that lives there, they will also remove one of the most important contributions to the local economy, the money brought in by visitors to the area.

The Smithsville Standard is right to say that local people are very concerned at these proposals. I have already been phoned by many people from the different local amenity societies who are all up in arms about the plans. We have formed a local campaign to preserve the downs.

I would be very grateful if you would be prepared to meet a group of us to discuss the plans and our objections to them in more detail. I hope you won't mind if I ring your office in the next few weeks to fix a brief appointment – three-quarters of an hour would probably suffice.

Yours sincerely

Cathy Smith, Co-ordinator, Smithsville Downs Preservation Campaign

The sample letter accepts that there is a need to improve local traffic problems, making it clear that the campaign is reasonable and not dogmatic; establishes that there is public concern about the issue by citing the local paper's viewpoint; makes it clear that the author speaks from a position of experience and reputation; cites the important and tangible argument about tourism, introducing a new dimension to the debate; and associates the campaign's name firmly with existing (amenity) organisations.

THE MEETING

You have fixed a meeting with your MP at the surgery. Now you must use the opportunity to get your case across.

- Select a small group of people, probably not more than four or five, who will be representative of your campaign and trusted by its members.
- Plan what each of them will say and do at the meeting. Appoint a leader who will ensure that all the key points that need to be made are made, and who will give everyone on your side the chance to speak. (People who do not want to say anything shouldn't be there, unless they are taking notes of the meeting. Giving everyone something to say ensures that people don't feel left out, lessening the chance of unscheduled and unhelpful interventions.)
- Appoint someone to take notes of the meeting and write them up later, particularly if you get promises of support – but also if you get a hostile response, so that you can ensure that you have replies to all the points made against you.
- Remember that even in the best-prepared delegation, there are occasions when mistakes are made. It is the responsibility of the leader of your side to correct, gently and unobtrusively, any unwitting mistake made by a member of your delegation. It is essential, however, to ensure that you have no public disagreements – mutual trust between members of your delegation is crucial, as is respect for your convenor.
- In order to rehearse your case for the final time, and to discuss together any new facts or new ideas for the meeting, ensure that your delegation has a pre-meeting before the actual meeting with your MP. This can ensure that each person is there to raise a different point.
- Prepare a short briefing on your argument to take with you to the meeting or send beforehand. If possible keep it to two sides of paper; keep it simple, outlining your case point by point; avoid jargon, unnecessary or unexplained statistics; and do not assume an understanding of initials or abbreviations.

Start your briefing with a short summary of what is written, go on to spell this out in a little more detail, and summarise what you wish your MP to do. Ensure this briefing is as presentable as possible, and certainly as presentable as anything else in your campaign: as with a press release or letter, type it neatly and ensure that it is copied cleanly on a good photocopier.

The main advantages of having a written briefing available are: it ensures that your MP has a reminder that he or she has promised to do something; it ensures that he or she has your arguments clearly expressed in your terms, rather than relying on notes of your arguments (an important difference); and you can use it for other purposes, such as a press release or as speech notes for your key activists.

- Unless your MP is already a convert, he or she will prefer to listen and take in your points rather than making a commitment to any rigid position. But do *not* let MPs get away without telling you what they intend to do. Remember, talking tends to expand to fill the time available – ensure that your delegation doesn't talk for so long that it is being shown the door with just a promise to 'think it over'.
- Remember, there is an opposing case to your own. Try to anticipate the arguments of your opponents and give your answers to these in the course of your meeting and in your written briefing.
- A meeting in the MP's surgery or office may be the most effective way of putting across a complicated case. But if you want to explain your case more graphically, then you may want to try to get your MP to come to you. This is particularly the case if your meeting is linked to a publicity opportunity – for example, Cathy Smith may want to have the local MPs come to the Smithsville Downs. Mrs Sheedy may wish to invite her councillors to the Smithsville Fields at night to check on the lights.

SMITHSVILLE DOWNS PRESERVATION CAMPAIGN

Sir Anthony Jones MP
House of Commons
London
SW1A 0AA

Dear Sir Anthony

It was good of you to meet us on Saturday to discuss the Smithsville Downs Preservation Campaign. We were very gratified to learn that you support our campaign so wholeheartedly.

We hope that your letter to the minister will draw a successful response, but we are very reassured by your determination to raise the matter through other parliamentary procedures if the response is not as forthcoming as we would hope.

We will of course be very pleased to help with any further information you should require.

Yours sincerely

Cathy Smith
Co-ordinator
Smithsville Downs Preservation Campaign

MP TO FIGHT FOR SMITHSVILLE DOWNS

Local Conservative MP Sir Anthony Jones is to join the fight to preserve Smithsville Downs, campaign co-ordinator Mrs Cathy Smith announced today.

Following a meeting with the Smithsville Downs Preservation Campaign, the MP is to write to the Secretary of State for Transport opposing plans to build a motorway link across the downs. He has promised to use all parliamentary channels to pursue the campaign if this initial response is negative.

Mrs Smith said today: 'We are very glad to welcome Sir Anthony's support. We have a very strong case made stronger by the support of both our local MPs. This shows the campaign is of concern to people of all parties who have the preservation of Smithsville Downs at heart.

'I have no doubt that we can win.'

Ends.

Note to editors: Smithsville East Labour MP Gavin Spiller declared his support for the campaign last week.

Further information: Colin Dennison, Publicity Officer, Smithsville Downs Preservation Campaign.

Telephone Smithsville 3377

OR

Cathy Smith, Co-ordinator of the Campaign.

Telephone Smithsville 2896

MP's VESTED INTEREST IN DOWNS MOTORWAY

Local Conservative MP Sir Anthony Jones was today condemned for putting vested interests before the preservation of Smithsville Downs. Campaign co-ordinator Mrs Cathy Smith said: 'Following a meeting with Sir Anthony we were disappointed to learn that his longstanding association with the roads lobby has blinded him to the beauty of the downs.

'In our meeting the campaign made it clear to Sir Anthony that there was great public concern about the future of the downs. Not only is a site of supreme natural beauty at stake, but the downs are one of our greatest tourist attractions. Driving a motorway through the downs will irreparably damage the local tourist industry.'

Mrs Smith said that the campaign would go ahead and welcomed the interest and support shown by Labour MP Gavin Spiller and by councillors from all political parties.

She added 'Sadly our Conservative MP is out of step with local opinion and his own local party. Several Conservative councillors have already pledged support for our campaign.'

ENDS

Further information: Colin Dennison, Publicity Officer, Smithsville Downs Preservation Campaign.

Telephone Smithsville 3377

OR

Cathy Smith, Co-ordinator of the Campaign

Telephone Smithsville 2896

- The most important action after the meeting is to write and thank your MP for meeting you, listing the action you believe he or she has agreed to take, and offering to help with further information should this be needed. This reminds him or her and acts as a reference for you. Obviously the letter will be based on the notes of the meeting taken by a member of your delegation and agreed by the rest of your delegation at your post-meeting debriefing.
- You may also wish to take the opportunity of publicising the result of your meeting. If you are going to issue a press release about your meeting, it is important to let your MP know this. If he or she is going to be credited with helping you, he or she will be gratified to know this. If your MP's response has been hostile, it is necessary that he or she should know that the issue will not go away.

WHAT YOUR MP CAN DO

Any effective MP knows that there are a variety of channels open to pursue an issue. While some may rely on behind-the-scenes lobbying, through contact with ministers – either through writing or taking a delegation to see a minister privately, or by bending the minister's ear in the queue to vote – there are also many public opportunities which campaigns that rely on public support and involvement need to know about. These devices are explained below for their publicity value.

The main parliamentary devices listed are used every day by MPs of all parties who are trying to advance a variety of different causes. They are:

- parliamentary questions, both written and oral;
- letters to ministers;
- early day motions;
- Standing Order No 20 applications;
- adjournment debates;
- private members' bills and private members' motions;
- hosting a meeting or lobby.

Parliamentary questions

These are the most common form of drawing an issue to the government's attention. Parliamentary questions fall into two categories: written and oral.

Sir Anthony Jones MP (Smithsville West)
House of Commons
London
SW1A 0AA

Mrs Z. Moriarty
Parliamentary Under-secretary
for Social Security
DSS

Dear Zena

Re: Pensioners and Housing Benefit

I attach a letter I have received from Mrs Augustine Kirkwood of Smithsville Pensioners Action Group concerning proposed cuts in housing benefit for pensioners.

I know Mrs Kirkwood well and I agree very strongly with the points she makes.

I would be very grateful for your comments.

Yours sincerely

Sir Anthony Jones

Hundreds of written questions may be tabled daily in the House of Commons on a variety of different subjects. They have to be specifically addressed to a particular government department which must have responsibility for action on the subject raised. They must be designed to draw out information from the government or ask for action. This information may be factual and statistical; or it may be an account of government policy on an issue or a minister's reasons for not pursuing a course of action or for pursuing a different course. Statistical information, particularly from the Department of Social Security and from the Treasury, can be invaluable to campaigns and pressure groups, providing a respectable source of information to be quoted back at government in a variety of documents, research, reports, press releases, articles and so on.

The number of parliamentary questions tabled on a particular subject can be an indicator of the level of concern a particular issue is arousing, particularly if the questions emanate from a variety of sources.

Oral questions, where a minister answers direct to the House of Commons, occur daily Monday to Thursday from 2.30 to 3.30 pm. Each government department is questioned on a rotating basis (always on the same day of the week), normally every four weeks or so.

The Prime Minister is questioned twice weekly for 15 minutes from 3.15 to 3.30 pm on Tuesdays and Thursdays.

In the House of Lords, there are four oral questions, known as 'starred questions', daily. These are allowed to range more widely in phraseology than House of Commons' questions, and they are not restricted to one or two departments each day.

Written question

Sir Anthony Jones: 'To ask the Secretary of State for Social Security how many pensioners will lose money as a result of the decision to adjust housing benefit payments.'

The Parliamentary Under-secretary for Social Security (Mrs Moriarty):

It is estimated that 2.9 million pensioners will have their housing benefit payments reduced but as this will be at the same time as the annual uprating of benefits none will lose cash.

Oral question

Mr Gavin Spiller asked the Secretary of State for Transport what representations he has received concerning the proposed Motorway link across Smithsville Downs.

The Secretary of State for Transport (Mr McIntosh): As a result of an organised lobby, some 70 representations have been received opposing the plans.

Mr Spiller: Does this not reflect the substantial public opposition in Smithsville to the monstrous plans which will destroy a site of quite outstanding natural beauty? Will the secretary of state not now take his plans away and reconsider?

Mr McIntosh: No, sir. The new motorway will promote employment for workers in the local construction industry, as well as improving communications with the south coast.

Sir Anthony Jones: Will my Rt Honourable Friend not accept that the concern that exists in Smithsville spreads across all political parties? Is he aware that the Smithsville Downs feature prominently in the English Tourist Board's publicity for the region? Are there not other routes that could be developed as alternatives, such as a third crossing over the River Thwaite?

Mr McIntosh: My Honourable Friend will be aware that there is to be a consultation process and we shall await its result with interest.

Hon Members: Humbug.

House of Lords Starred Question

Lord Stamford of Smithsville: My Lords, I beg leave to ask the question standing in my name upon the order paper.

The question was as follows:

To ask Her Majesty's Government whether they have given further consideration to alternative plans for the new motorway link to the south coast.

(This would then continue as with a Commons' oral question.)

In the House of Commons most oral questions tend to be fairly simple. They are 'tabled' two weeks before being asked, and so have to be capable of being topical when eventually they are answered. Generally speaking, they are a peg on which to hang a supplementary question. Each MP asking an oral question (generally only the first 15 or so are reached) has the opportunity to ask a supplementary question and then other MPs are allowed to ask questions on the same subject before the Speaker moves on to the next tabled question.

Letters to ministers

If you or I write to a minister about a subject, it is likely that we will receive replies from a junior civil servant. If an MP writes to a minister they receive a reply from the minister. Government departments, particularly departments such as the Department of Social Security, receive thousands of letters from MPs every year. On topical issues such as social security cuts the replies will be largely standardised with merely the first line different. But each letter from an MP will be seen by the relevant minister, who will at least be alerted to the degree of concern being expressed by MPs.

Early day motions

Early day motions are a kind of MPs' petition. They are a way for backbench MPs to express concern about an issue. Each parliamentary session several hundred EDMs (so called because time is requested for them to be debated at the earliest day available) are tabled on every subject possible. Each EDM can have up to six sponsors whose names appear with the motion on every day after a new MP has added his name to the motion.

EDMs are rarely debated. The rare occasions when they are debated tend to be when the opposition, noticing that a government MP has tabled an EDM criticising the government on a controversial or topical issue, uses its own time to produce for debate a motion almost identical to the EDM already tabled (it cannot be absolutely identical for procedural reasons) in the hope of getting government members to vote with it.

EDMs are a useful indication of parliamentary support for a particular position and can often attract several hundred signatories. Government whips are particularly sensitive to EDMs. They are drawn to the attention of the relevant minister and also to the Leader of the House, for whom briefs are prepared in case an MP asks whether the government will find time to debate an EDM when questions are raised on the forthcoming week's business each Thursday.

Like parliamentary questions, EDMs are a good vehicle for publicity.

EDM 632 PRESERVATION OF SMITHSVILLE DOWNS

Sir Anthony Jones
Mr Gavin Spiller

That this House urges Her Majesty's Government to find an alternative route for the new south-coast motorway link, possibly by creating a third River Thwaite crossing, and congratulates the Smithsville Downs Preservation Campaign on its vigorous campaign to protect this site of outstanding natural beauty.

As an amendment to Sir Anthony Jones' proposed motion
Mr Donald Bunting: after 'link', insert 'but not through Little Smithsville'.

EDM 100 PROTECTION OF PENSIONERS' HOUSING BENEFIT

Sir Anthony Jones

That this House urges Her Majesty's Government to drop its plans to reduce pensioners' entitlement to housing benefit.

EDM 777 FREEDOM OF INFORMATION BILL

Mr Gavin Spiller

That this House urges the immediate introduction of Freedom of Information legislation along the lines advocated by the Freedom of Information Campaign.

Standing Order No 20 applications

Standing Order No 20 allows MPs to move the adjournment of the business of the House of Commons for the day or day following that on which they make the application. It is very rarely that the Speaker allows such an application, which has to be on a subject that is specific and important and needs urgent consideration.

A recent example where this device did lead to a debate was on 24 June 1993, when the government announced its decision on the award of the refitting contract for the Trident submarine. The opposition front bench made a Standing Order No 20 application, and the debate took place the same evening.

This device is often used by MPs wishing to draw attention to a topical matter.

Adjournment debates

The last item of business each day in the House of Commons is an adjournment debate. Subjects for debate are chosen by the Speaker, and a variety of different subjects crop up each week. (The Smithsville Downs motorway link would have a good chance.)

In an adjournment debate an MP gets the opportunity to speak for 15 minutes and the relevant junior minister replies for the same length of time. This allows quite an in-depth examination of a subject, during which time the government has to put its case on record. Most of these debates, of course, take place late at night, and are not therefore a good opportunity for media coverage nationally, but they can be followed up locally. Friday's debates take place in the afternoon, and so may have more chance of being noticed. MPs introducing adjournment debates may, if they wish, give up some of their own time to allow other MPs to contribute on the same subject before the minister replies.

There are special times for adjournment debates before the recesses, and also opportunities to raise subjects on the motion for the recess (during which time MPs can explain that the House should not rise before a particular subject has been discussed – the Leader of the House replies to this).

Private members' bills and private members' motions

Private members' bills fall into three main types – the ballotted private members' bills, ten minute rule bills and bills which are merely presented before the House.

Early in the new session of parliament there is a ballot amongst MPs for the opportunity to introduce a *private members' bill*. Those whose names are chosen have the opportunity to introduce a private members' bill, for which time will be allowed on the floor of the House. Usually only the top six MPs have any *real* chance of seeing the bill they choose pass into law, and these are lobbied intensively by a variety of pressure groups. Time is set aside on Fridays for these bills which go through the full course of legislative stages as with any other law passed by parliament. Such bills are usually – but not always – specific, short and relatively uncontroversial.

Additionally, each Tuesday, Wednesday and Thursday, MPs have the opportunity under the *ten minute rule* to seek leave to introduce a bill. These *ten minute rule bills* never get anywhere, but they are an opportunity to highlight an issue. Publicity-wise, they occur at a key moment, just after question time and before the main afternoon debate, when there are still journalists present in the gallery. The procedure is that an MP speaks for ten minutes on why a particular bill is needed. More often than not the bill is unopposed. An MP wishing to oppose it is also allowed ten minutes and then a vote is taken.

MPs may also present draft bills to the House and these are allowed to be printed without any opportunity to speak on the bill.

Private members' motions are ballotted and take place on some Fridays. Again, almost any subject can be debated, though this would normally need to be wider than just a constituency matter. Again it is an opportunity for an MP to get a response from a government minister who may well have to participate in the debate.

Hosting a meeting or lobby

There are a number of meeting rooms in the Palace of Westminster which MPs can book for outside meetings. The most likely experience your campaign will have of meetings at the House of Commons will be as part of a mass lobby, probably organised by the national campaign to which you may be affiliated. As part of the campaign to protect pensioners' incomes, Augustine Kirkwood's Smithsville Pensioners Action Group would join a mass lobby organised by an alliance of pensioners' groups and charities concerned with the welfare of elderly people.

ORGANISING A MASS LOBBY OF PARLIAMENT

Mass lobbies need to be held when most MPs are likely to be at Westminster; that is, on Tuesday, Wednesday or Thursday. Tuesday and Thursday are often the best days, since Prime Minister's question time takes place on those days and important lobbies are likely to receive a mention during it, ensuring valuable extra publicity – including a useful additional angle for television coverage on the lobby.

Arrangements for mass lobbies are orchestrated with the Ceremonials Office at Cannon Row Police Station, which will be aware of any lobbies already booked. The inspector in charge at Cannon Row, the coaches branch of the police and the Serjeant at Arms Office at the Palace of Westminster need to be informed about your lobby.

There are normally two distinct features to mass lobbies: the first is a meeting or series of meetings in the Grand Committee Room; the second is the opportunity for local groups to lobby their own MP.

The Grand Committee Room has to be booked by an MP and an MP has to be there at the start of the meeting. An MP should be present throughout, though not necessarily the MP who booked the meeting. In any case you will want an MP to chair your meeting in the Grand Committee Room. The Grand Committee Room holds about 200 people, so a sizeable lobby will mean you holding three shortish meetings in order to involve as many people as possible.

The police will help you to run your meeting in shifts, letting in one audience and letting another out.

You will have publicised your lobby by letter to MPs you are anxious to attract and, by getting an insert in the all-party whip produced between the government and opposition whips' offices and in the House magazine, you can expect a number of MPs to drop in for parts of the time. Some will speak at your meeting, but make sure you get a list of all those who turn up to your meetings for follow-up purposes later.

Other meetings can be held with the co-operation of other MPs in other rooms. Alternatively you may want to hold a rally for a larger number of people than the Grand Committee Room can hold. The closest venue is Central Hall, Westminster.

Ensure that you convey a sense of participation amongst all those attending the lobby, preferably by producing publicity material including stickers or badges, briefings to assist their own lobbying and so on.

PENSIONERS LOBBY 31 JANUARY 1985

Instructions to local groups

Final details for groups attending the mass lobby are as follows:

1 Ensure that you have booked an appointment with your MP. If possible, arrange that he or she will collect you from the queue outside the House of Commons. Otherwise you will have to wait to be let into the Palace of Westminster.

2 If you have been unable to fix an appointment with your MP, you will have to join the queue outside the House of Commons in the normal manner. When you are allowed into the building to the Central Lobby you will fill in a green card which will be taken by staff of the House of Commons who will attempt to find your MP. Be warned that this will take some time!

3 The lobby starts at 2.15. You can come and queue up before then, but you will not be let into the building. We expect the lobby to end around 5.00.

4 There will be a series of meetings in the Grand Committee Room in the Palace of Westminster and you will probably find yourself attending one of these meetings while waiting to see your MP.

5 You must not bring placards or banners as these are not allowed within a mile radius of the House of Commons.

6 If you are coming by coach please let us know immediately so that we can give a firm figure on the number of coaches to the police coaches branch.

7 Coaches can drop off at the Embankment. Ensure that all the members of your delegation know where your pick-up point is.

8 We have appointed several stewards, who will be distinguished by blue armbands. Please obey their instructions at all times. We will have stewards outside with the queue, in the Grand Committee Room and in the Central Lobby.

9 We will be producing briefing notes for all those attending the lobby, as well as stickers and badges. If there are particular examples of pensioners' poverty from your locality, including surveys, please bring this information with you.

10 Don't forget to let your local papers, TV and radio know that you are attending the lobby.

YOUR COUNCILLORS

Most of the techniques so far described with reference to MPs can be applied to making approaches to councillors. But if you want your councillors to act for you, there are a further series of questions you need to ask yourself.

Which council is responsible for taking the decision?

At present we are going through one of the periodic reforms of local government, and responsibilities for certain services may change. The government is seeking to obtain a reorganisation of councils into single tiers that are responsible for all functions. In Wales and Scotland, announcements of an overall structure have already been made. In England, the Local Government Commission is adjudicating on a community-by-community basis. It is not possible at the time of writing to give clear and firm guidelines as the distinctions between different tiers are being blurred across the country.

If you are uncertain as to which council to approach, you may be able to work this out from a local library.

Which councillors are involved and which do you want to involve?

The Local Government (Access to Information) Act 1985 requires councils to publish a list of councillors' names and wards and the public's rights to information. The Council Information Office ought to be able to furnish you with a list of council committee membership. This may be available in the reference library. Most local authorities publish a yearbook with details of all councillors and their committees. This should also give their home addresses, but if not you can get these from the *Municipal Yearbook* in your local library. Many councils also have a list of members' financial interests. Contact the chief executive's office for this.

Let's use two Smithsville campaigns to make our point. Both Brian Hunter of the Smithsville Housing Action Committee and Marie Sheedy who is trying to improve the lighting need to lobby their local council.

The full council meeting has taken the decision to go ahead with the new municipal buildings. The decision has now been given to a subcommittee to consider in more detail. Brian Hunter is not too interested in this subcommittee: its role is to work out the plans for the new buildings, not to consider whether the decisions are right. Any reversal of the decision will have to occur at the full council meeting.

Brian already has a number of contacts amongst councillors. The chairperson of the council housing committee sits on the management committee of the Smithsville Housing Action Committee, as do two other members of the housing committee. Smithsville, being a balanced council, has nominated members from all three parties to most of the committees on which the council is represented. Brian naturally feels that the housing committee members are likely to be the most sympathetic to his objective and he determines to contact them individually, starting with the chairperson.

He knows, however, that one or two of the councillors on the housing committee are also enthusiastic members of the subcommittee examining plans for the new building. Remember these conflicts of interest!

Marie Sheedy has already written to the council department responsible for lighting in Smithsville Fields, and has received a reply from an officer. She wants to make the point that this is the fifth time this has happened in six months. Marie determines to get in touch with her local councillor. She has seen a list of local councillors for the area at the library and knows that her councillors hold a surgery at Lower Smithsville School every Saturday. In any case her local councillors are very active, and their regular newsletter comes through her door every month, with their home telephone numbers in it. She rings up to make sure that they will be there.

Which departments are involved?

Each council is split into separate departments. Their addresses are listed in the telephone directory. A quick call to the relevant department will tell you the name of its head. It is always worth going to the top if you want something done – and letting whoever you speak to know you are contacting your councillor at the same time.

Which committees and subcommittees are involved?

As Brian Hunter has already found out, different committees, subcommittees and the full council are involved in different decisions. To plan your campaign effectively, you need to know the date, time and place of meeting of all the relevant bodies discussing the matter. All the meetings should be open to the public (following pressure from the Campaign for Freedom of Information).

It is important to keep in touch with the committee meetings and council meetings, even when all that is happening is a brief report on progress. Each occasion may provide you with an invaluable opportunity for getting further press coverage for your case. Ensure that one member of your campaign, possibly on a rota basis, attends each relevant meeting.

The passing of the Local Government (Access to Information) Act 1985 extended the public's rights to attend council meetings. Previously the public only had the right of access legally to full council meetings and council committee meetings. The Act also gives members of the public the right to inspect agendas and reports of council meetings, committees or subcommittees and, subject to the payment of a reasonable charge, to inspect all background papers relating to agenda items.

Full council meetings may have one or two matters of heated and controversial debate, but generally their business is taken up with ratifying the decisions of council committee meetings. A councillor wishing to raise or challenge a meeting of a relevant subcommittee or committee may do so at full council.

It is useful to know the council's standing orders if you are trying to influence a decision. The standing orders outline the procedures of the council's business. They should be in your local reference library, and a friendly local councillor should be able to advise on them. Standing orders may grant the public additional rights to those legally guaranteed – they cannot undermine your legal right of access to information.

You will find that many decisions taken at committee or subcommittee level are really only an endorsement of a recommendation made by the relevant officer and chairperson of the committee. They are two people whose support can be critical as they have real power to influence decisions.

Once you have lobbied the members of the key committee, you should have managed to locate a sympathetic councillor who will be able to tip you off about forthcoming meetings and any internal rumours.

Does the council have an overwhelming political bias in one direction, or is it a balanced council?

If no party has an overall majority, the opportunity for pressure groups and campaigns to gain support on the merits of their case is increased. No party will want to offend public opinion on a sensitive issue in such a situation if they can avoid it, and the political impact of your case will be strengthened. You may be able to involve party officials in putting pressure on their councillors with more success in such a situation.

Does your council receive deputations?

Some councils have special provisions for receiving deputations. This can be an effective adjunct to your other lobbying activities.

Deputations are allowed to address a council meeting prior to its discussion of a subject. If you are organising a deputation it is best to wait until you have lobbied a number of councillors and know you have some 'friends' in the council chamber.

If you want to send a deputation, get in touch with your council and speak to the department responsible for committee administration to check on arrangements. Make sure you know how long you are allowed to speak for and how many people are entitled to go. It is essential that your case is well presented, so use your best public speaker. You may have to answer questions from councillors, so be well prepared. See S for Speeches on pages 72 to 74.

Let the press know that you will be sending a deputation and that members will be available for interview. Your supporters may want to come – make sure you find out how many people can fit into the public gallery of your council to avoid disappointment.

LOBBYING – AN AFTERWORD

Above all when lobbying, be polite, listen intently to the person you are lobbying, and try to pick up his or her real feelings about the issue. Some politicians are very good at just being a member of the parliamentary or municipal 'club' – they may sound sympathetic, but really only want a quiet life and the status of office. On the other hand, many politicians are dedicated, committed and sensitive to public opinion. Many are massively overworked and most will be grateful that you have taken the time to plan your case so that you save them time and energy.

Part Three

The Results

5 Case History: CLEAR

... a pressure group success story

On Sunday, 24 January 1982, a news story appeared in *The Observer*. It stated that a campaign for lead-free petrol was to be launched the following day – 'the biggest environmental campaign for years'. Although it said 'details are being kept secret,' it contained just enough information to whet the appetite. The story was planted by me in a deliberate leak to convey to the rest of the media that they should take notice of a press conference that coming Monday. It was a mini-exercise in hype justified by events, for this was the beginning of a pressure group campaign that was in 15 months to take on and defeat some of the most powerful multi-national industries – the petroleum industry, the car manufacturers, the lead industry – and ministers and civil servants, and was to achieve a spectacular victory with a reversal of national policy and a decision in principle to move to lead-free petrol.

In the course of the campaign almost all of the techniques outlined in this book were employed, and I tell this story not for glory but because I think it is both a useful illustration of how to run a single-issue campaign of this kind and hopefully a source of encouragement to others.

Let's start at the beginning – with the problem itself. Lead is a neurotoxin – a brain poison. Excessive exposure to lead can cause serious illness and even death. Until fairly recently it was assumed that at everyday levels of exposure – that is, at blood lead levels of 35 micrograms per decilitre (μg/dl) or less – no harm would be caused, and this has been the justification for its continued widespread use in paint, in water piping and, above all, in petrol. Recently, however, a number of scientists in different countries, including the United States, Great Britain, Australia and Germany, have produced evidence to suggest that children could be adversely affected at much lower levels of exposure than previously realised and are at risk of reduced IQ, learning difficulties because they are easily distracted or frustrated and other behavioural problems at levels of 10–15 μg/dl or even less.

Now, I must emphasise that the scientific world was and still is divided on the issue. There have been studies that reinforce the fears, and studies that fail to confirm them. The issue increasingly was whether we could ever achieve 'conclusive' evidence of harm. And, second, how many children had to be exposed to risk until the issue was scientifically settled? Those who believed that lead exposure at these lower levels did damage children took the view that urgent action should be taken to reduce exposure. Those who were unconvinced about the dangers took the view that the necessary action did not justify the cost and inconvenience involved.

In the USA, the Environmental Protection Agency decided that the evidence of a *risk* to health represented sufficient grounds for action, and decided as far back as 1970 that it made sense to remove lead from petrol. There was an additional argument for this: namely, that they wished to introduce catalytic converters to cars to control other emissions, and lead damages the converters. So for *both* reasons they ruled that all new cars coming on the market from 1975 should run on lead-free petrol, and that lead-free petrol should be available at all petrol stations. Japan and Australia were also going lead-free.

The Americans had also virtually banned lead in paint used in domestic circumstances – their maximum permitted level is 660 parts per million (ppm). In Britain, however, there were no controls whatsoever, although there was a voluntary understanding between the paint manufacturers and the authorities that there would be warning notices on all paint containing more than 5,000 ppm. The comparison was astonishing – in Britain the lead content of a tin of paint has to be over eight times that permitted in the USA before even a warning label is required!

Over the years tougher action had been taken in Britain over lead in water pipes, although there were still many old houses with leaded water pipes and there was still some use of lead in solder.

Food can manufacturers in Britain announced in 1983 that as a result of the CLEAR campaign they were going to eliminate the use of lead in solder and in the manufacture of their product altogether.

But to return to lead in petrol, the position at the beginning of 1981 was that Britain was permitting 0.40 grams of lead per litre of petrol and the car manufacturers and the petroleum industry hoped that this would continue. There was, however, increasing concern about the health risk, much of it motivated by the Conservation Society, which set up a special working party, and a small number of scientists, notably Dr Robert Stephens of the University of Birmingham and Professor Derek Bryce-Smith of the University of Reading. A report by a DHSS working party, chaired by Professor Patrick Lawther, had recommended a number of steps to reduce lead exposure but had fallen short of recommending lead-free petrol. The minister concerned, Tom King at the Department of the Environment, finally decided on the basis of the Lawther report and under the influence of pressure from the industries, to reject lead-free petrol, and in May 1981 he announced in the House of Commons a compromise measure, namely reduction to 0.15 grams per litre by the mid-1980s. Given the strength of the Conservative administration, and the Lawther report, it looked as if the anti-lead lobby was defeated and the possibility of lead-free petrol in this century appeared to be virtually nil. It was hardly the best time to launch a major campaign for lead-free petrol, and yet this was the background to the launch of CLEAR.

At this point we introduce to the story Mr Godfrey Bradman. The wealthy chairman of a public company, he had lived with his family in Chelsea. Always sensitive to any threat to the health of his children, he had become concerned by occasional articles he had read about the emission of lead from car exhausts, and especially about the heavy traffic in the vicinity of his home. He decided to explore the issue for himself and went to considerable lengths, including meeting Lawther and studying books on the subject. His conclusion was that the risk was too considerable to be ignored, and his first step was to move his family home out of the centre of London. Fortunately, Godfrey Bradman is not the kind of man to look after himself and his family and not care about anyone else. He began talking to members of the Conservation Society working party and others and offered to fund a fresh campaign. They advertised for a director.

While this was happening I was employed as deputy editor of the *Illustrated London News*, and one of my responsibilities was to cover the affairs of the capital itself. I decided to explore the problems of pollution caused by heavy traffic. This took me to the lead question and I was directed to Godfrey Bradman. He told me of his campaign and as we talked he convinced me that the problem warranted serious investigation, while I convinced him that his plans for a campaign of the 'corridors of power' were unrealistic and that what was required was a major public campaign. It was to be the beginning of a close friendship and an effective working partnership. He persuaded me to meet his advisers, who were at that time interviewing for the director, and the end result was an invitation to me to run the campaign as its full-time chairman. I was still doubtful, however, and spent some time attempting to investigate the problem further. The more I looked at it, the more it seemed to be a classic case of multi-national industries with enormous economic and political power ruthlessly persisting with a potentially hazardous practice with complete indifference to its health effects; of the close relations between these industries and Whitehall meaning that the industrial point of view carried far greater clout than the concern of ordinary people; and of apathy and compromise instead of the kind of decisive action with a built-in bias towards the public that we should expect from the authorities we elect to protect public health. My research convinced me that there was an overwhelming case for the elimination of lead from petrol – and for measures to reduce lead in paint and lead in water piping – because of the *risk* to children.

However, there was another point and, given the confusion over the health evidence, it was the one that finally convinced me that action should be taken. (The Royal Commission on Environmental Pollution was some two years later to give priority to the same point.) This was that lead was non-degradable. In other words, unlike many other environmental pollutants, it does not disappear eventually. It just builds up and builds up around us. We produce and add to that build-up over 3.5 million tonnes every year. Scientists have demonstrated that the lead in our bodies is already in the vicinity of 500 times higher than natural levels – that the industrial exploitation of lead has led to its widespread dissemination all over the globe so that it is in the air we breathe, in the dust children pick up on their fingers, in the water we drink and in our food. Even if it could be proved that children have so far not been damaged – and I doubt if that can be proved – it is clear that as more and more of this poison accumulates around us, we are building up for generations to come a legacy of pollution that will have devastating effects. There was, therefore, a long-term environmental case for action. The problem, however, was how to persuade a government which prided itself on the 'resolute approach' to change its mind so soon after it had proudly announced what it believed to be an adequate measure. Another problem was how to overcome the resources of finance and influence of these big industries. From the start, I was convinced that there was no point in detailed argument and negotiation unless it took place from a background of overwhelming public concern. We had to politicise the issue.

We decided, therefore, on a major campaign on the health question. We would refuse to become involved in arguments with industry over the costs and technical problems of the introduction of lead-free petrol. We would simply rest our case on the fact that the Americans and the Japanese had conclusively proved that it could be done, and had done it without much additional cost or loss of energy resources. We would not allow industry to deflect the argument on to ground where they could be most effective and into territory where they controlled all of the information (or misinformation). We would argue our case on health and long-term environmental grounds alone; once the decision was taken we could involve ourselves, if necessary, in the secondary debate about how it should be done and at what cost.

This was a crucial initial decision, and throughout the 15 months of the campaign the industry tried to move us off our own ground and on to theirs, but we steadfastly refused to be drawn. I believe this policy was a key factor in our success. That decision taken, we moved to our objectives. I have explained fully (see A for Aims on pages 24 to 26) the importance of establishing clear and realistic objectives and how we set about this exercise for CLEAR.

Once we had decided on the ground on which we would fight and on our objectives, the next steps were to set up the campaign in structural and financial terms. Godfrey Bradman had been incredibly generous, making available a budget of over £100,000 to finance the launch and build-up of the campaign. Clearly few pressure groups have an advantage such as this, and I fully acknowledge that without it we could never have won as quickly as we did. I do believe we would still have achieved our objectives, but it would have taken longer and been much harder work. I have always taken the view, however, that no campaign should be dependent on only one source of income. Inevitably there is a vulnerability in that position. Therefore, I made it our aim to try to match the Bradman input with money from other sources – donations from the public, fund-raising events, contributions by other organisations, grants by trusts for research and so on. I didn't achieve a 50:50 breakdown during the CLEAR campaign, but we did raise around 40 per cent of the total budget from other sources, some of it with Godfrey Bradman's help in terms of contacts or underwriting of appeals.

Finance, therefore, was not going to be a major problem in the early days, and the pre-launch period was used for research, the preparation of first-class print material and the creation of the coalition. (The necessity and the techniques for each of these are described in Chapter 3; see pages 85 to 131.) We assembled filing cabinets of reports, studies and books on lead pollution, and examined them carefully in order to demonstrate to ourselves the strength of the case and to be in a position to demonstrate it to others. We considered all of the arguments of the other side and established convincing answers. We slowly developed a solid scientific case based on the best studies and on a relatively cautious interpretation of those studies. We were determined not to overstate the case, and in this respect we expected to compare favourably with some earlier campaigners and thus wrong-foot our opposition.

We decided to take advantage of Godfrey Bradman's generosity to produce print material of a much higher quality than would normally have been possible or necessary. The justification was that when we launched the campaign we could present our evidence in a highly impressive and professional manner in order to undermine the charge that we were just a bunch of cranks. We produced a first-class newspaper and handbook for publication at the time of the launch.

It was because of this need to destroy the image of being a small, emotional minority that we set about building a coalition with other organisations and compiling a list of supporters to give the campaign a substance that would make it difficult to brush it aside lightly. We set up a charitable trust, and recruited such public figures as Dame Elizabeth Ackroyd, former director of the Consumer Council; trade unionist Clive Jenkins; conservationist Lord Avebury; Dr David Bellamy; Jonathan Miller; former Whitehall adviser Professor Christopher Foster; and influential journalist Sheila Black. Invitations for the launch were issued by eight national organisations. By that time we already had 130 MPs in support, for in order to achieve maximum political support from the start we had circulated to all MPs our objectives, together with a form for them to sign indicating their support. In addition, I went to see Dr David Owen, parliamentary leader of the SDP, and wrote to Liberal leader David Steel and Labour leader Michael Foot; all replied with supportive letters that we were able to quote at the launch of our campaign. We ultimately built the list of supporting MPs to well over 200 by writing a second time to those who had not replied to the first letter and even arranging for some MPs to collect signatures on our behalf.

So we came to January 1982, with the date of the launch fixed for Monday, 25 January. It was in January that we received the Yellowlees letter and took the decision not to employ it at the opening press conference (see Y for Yellowlees on pages 81 to 84). It did, however, enormously strengthen our confidence, for it was useful to know that when we walked into the press conference on 25 January we had in our pockets a complete answer to those who might say that there was no high-level medical opinion behind the CLEAR case.

In addition to sending out invitations to the media for the press conference, we made a point of identifying those journalists who had written about the issue before, and giving them personal briefings in advance so that they would feel particularly involved and give it priority. In addition, we met with Geoffrey Lean of *The Observer*, who had been campaigning on the issue in *The Observer*'s columns for a couple of years. Geoffrey was naturally keen to publish an item on the Sunday before the launch rather than follow the national newspapers some six days later. It is in circumstances like these that trust and understanding between a journalist and campaigner are essential. We decided it would be helpful to the campaign to have a small apparent 'leak' in *The Observer*, and provided Lean with just enough information for him to be able to build a story but not so much that journalists at the press conference the next day would feel that they had been cheated. Thus, Lean did not have the right to publish the fact that the three party leaders were supporting the campaign, or that the number of MPs involved was in fact approaching 140, or the precise objectives of the campaign, or the details of two additional studies we were publicising at the launch. He was, however, able to hint that there was considerable political support and to say that two studies would be published. Thus, all sides were happy; we got the necessary build-up to our campaign; Lean got the exclusive story about the forthcoming launch of the campaign; and none of the media the following day felt that the story had been pre-empted.

The press conference took place in a building in Westminster Square at 11.00 am on Monday, 25 January, and for an hour beforehand we were giving radio and television interviews. It was well attended and the publicity was widespread. We were under way.

On the same day as the press conference we mailed to all MPs, and to other organisations and influential parties, copies of the handbook and the newspaper.

Not only did we receive widespread news coverage but also considerable support in leading articles, both in national and provincial newspapers. The *Guardian* in a leader stated, 'When there is such widespread feeling in favour of a reform, and a cleaner air bonus at the end of it, the government can be accused of obstinacy – and worse – in selecting this question as one on which to dig in its heels.' *The Observer* stated that ministers should:

> insist that new cars sold by 1985 – or soon after – should use leadless fuel ... unless overwhelming new evidence emerges to show that there is no danger to children. Their health, and their future contribution to the country must have priority over all other considerations.

By now we had created a small, united and professional team to run the campaign. We had taken a small, top-floor office in a building near King's Cross, staffed by myself and by two colleagues, Susan Dibb, administrator of the campaign, and Patricia Simms, who acted as research assistant/PA. Our two top volunteer helpers and advisers were Dr Robin Russell Jones and Dr Robert Stephens. The latter, as I have mentioned, had been campaigning on the issue for some time and his speciality was the environmental build-up of lead. Robin Russell Jones, who like Godfrey Bradman had moved his family out of London because of the problem, had made an extensive study of the health evidence. Throughout the campaign these two were to advise and speak on these two subjects, leaving the politics to me.

Immediately after the London launch the three of us set off on a provincial tour, holding receptions and making presentations in Coventry, Birmingham, Manchester, Liverpool, Leeds, Newcastle, Bristol, Southampton and Cardiff. These cities were chosen because they are media centres, each with television stations covering the surrounding counties. The aim of the provincial tours was to achieve widespread publicity throughout the country at local level, to meet local environmental health officers and others and inform them of our activities, and to build up local support and identify people who could represent the campaign at local level.

While we were on the tour, we watched closely what was happening in the national media, where the petroleum industry and car manufacturers were trying to fight back, either with scare stories about the cost of lead-free petrol or claims that there was no health hazard. On 3 February we were in Liverpool and it was there that we decided the time was coming to play our trump card – the Yellowlees letter. (The full story of the leak of the Yellowlees letter has been told in Y for Yellowlees on pages 81 to 84.) The impact was beyond my wildest dreams. The news story in *The Times*, and my article opposite the leader page, set the rest of the media off, and that night the *Evening Standard* published a leader supporting the campaign. By Tuesday the matter was on the floor of the House of Commons and the Prime Minister herself was faced with the issue by both David Steel and Michael Foot. Up to this point the CLEAR campaign had been well received; after the publication of the Yellowlees letter it became a genuinely popular cause, with letters of support and money flooding in and almost 100 per cent medical backing. The number of MPs who had signed up as supporters increased dramatically.

It was crucial to maintain the momentum. Back in 1981 Godfrey Bradman had commissioned the City firm of Coopers and Lybrand to look at the issue and I had for some time had their report. Its value was not only the view that it presented, that it would have been possible to introduce lead-free petrol, but also the firm's reputation – no one could possibly describe such a reputable company as emotional. Nevertheless, and perhaps injudiciously from the firm's point of view, the authors of the report had actually stated that not to take every reasonable precaution would be 'criminal'. So a few days after the publication of the Yellowlees letter I called a small press conference in my office for just five newspapers and a representative of the PA, briefed them on the Coopers and Lybrand report and gave them a copy. Reports appeared in all the main national newspapers and all over the country and once more lead-free petrol was in the news.

What was happening was a bandwagon effect: first the launch of the campaign, then the Yellowlees letter, then the Coopers and Lybrand report – the impression was of an irresistible force building up. We worked hard to maintain this momentum. The next step was to persuade a Conservative Member of the European Parliament, Stanley Johnson – who was on the European Parliament environmental committee – to table a motion calling for lead-free petrol and the CLEAR objectives. The publication of this, and the suggestion that the issue would now become a European one, attracted another round of publicity. About this time we took our full-page ad in *The Observer*. This not only raised money and developed our list of supporters still further, but also led to several radio and television producers and other journalists deciding they wanted to take a closer look at the issue. Thus we achieved even more publicity.

While all this was going on, we had commissioned the MORI organisation to conduct an opinion poll and when Bob Worcester, the chairman of MORI, telephoned me he said even he could hardly believe the results. 'They are some of the most decisive figures I have ever seen,' he told me. And indeed they were – nine out of ten people wanted lead out of petrol, and 77 per cent said they wanted action even if petrol prices went up by 'a few pence per gallon'. (See O for Opinion Polls on pages 64 to 66 for details of the arrangement we made for its publication in *The Observer*.) That Saturday night I was in the centre of London and, knowing *The Observer* could be purchased at that time, I picked one up. I quickly looked at the front page and could see no report on our opinion poll. I looked at the other news pages and it wasn't there either. I could hardly believe it. Had we been let down? I looked back at the front page and then realised why I had missed it – it was the *front-page lead* and even I had not expected that. I had not even looked at the main headline on the front page. By now BBC Radio was leading its news with the story from *The Observer*, and all the national newspapers ran results of the poll the following Monday. *The Observer*'s leader said:

> The poll ... vindicates the campaign's objectives and pays tribute to the skill with which it is being conducted. ... The one substantial question for the government to resolve is whether society is prepared to accept some inconvenience to the car industry and a few more pence on a gallon of petrol to protect its children. After today's poll there can be no further doubt that it is, and the government should hesitate no longer.

The *Guardian* also ran a leader in support. *The Daily Telegraph* headed its story with the fact that the government was 'losing the argument'.

We had now succeeded in maintaining the momentum for over six weeks and both the industries and the government must have wondered how long we could sustain it. It was an issue that concerned me as well. However, a campaign can create its own luck, and the bandwagon effect had been such that it almost developed its own momentum. We were given a boost by the disclosure that the board of science of the British Medical Association had voiced its concern: 'The Board believes that all sources of lead pollution should be eliminated wherever possible.' Then we received another leak – this time a British Petroleum internal briefing document that actually disclosed that oil companies had secretly recommended lead-free petrol a year earlier and their offer had been declined by the authorities. We were also helped by the staggering incompetence of our main opponents, the Associated Octel Company, who persisted in getting different members of the staff to write letters to *The Financial Times* and the *Guardian* raising the issue and presenting their case. This simply set up opportunities for us to reply, and thus they helped sustain the debate and controversy.

At this point it is worth pausing to examine how the opposition reacted to our campaign. Perhaps their biggest blunder occurred before the campaign was even launched. In early November 1981 we wrote to ten leading British oil companies stating that we were 'concerned about the growing body of evidence of a serious health hazard arising from the use of lead in petrol,' and seeking further clarification of the individual companies' position and the answers to a number of technical questions. We also requested that the companies meet a deputation to discuss the issue further. Had they been well advised, they would have answered the questions honestly, even knowing that the answers would be unsatisfactory, and would have received a deputation. It was no secret that a campaign was planned, and this offered them the opportunity to make acquaintance with the campaigners, to seek to achieve some dialogue or minimal common ground, or at least to communicate their point of view. Instead, not one of the companies would answer the questions or meet the deputation; every one of the ten companies wrote an almost identical letter saying that we would be answered by the UK Petroleum Industry Association. The association took ten weeks to reply and their answer was a public relations brush-off.

This was a disastrous error for the petroleum industry, for throughout our campaign we were able to demonstrate that we had attempted to establish a dialogue and to hear the industrial case and been denied adequate answers or an audience. This, together with the unanswerable evidence that this response was orchestrated, strengthened our charges that the industry was only concerned to organise a cover-up. The petroleum industry did not help itself by its panicky claims of the high cost of lead-free petrol, often contradicted by other companies and undoubtedly contradicted by the American and Japanese experience. Nor was it helped by the leak that showed it had recommended lead-free petrol and then for a year kept quiet about it.

On the whole, the petroleum industry tried to avoid the health debate altogether, claiming that this was not within their area of expertise. CLEAR replied that no manufacturer or producer had the right to adopt a position of neutrality on the safety of its product. As I wrote in *The Lead Scandal*:

> It has a responsibility to be fully involved, to explore the health risk it creates, and to enter the debate on it. If it does not, it is in effect saying

> that its concern is the making of money, and responsibility for the health of human beings belongs elsewhere. No individual, no company, can properly assume such a position.

On the whole the petroleum industry was happy to leave the Associated Octel Company, manufacturers of the lead additives, to fight the battle on its behalf. Associated Octel's early response to CLEAR was to produce its own print material claiming there was no problem, and quoting all sorts of people out of context. For instance, the *British Medical Journal* had published a leader stating, 'The BMJ believes there is a good case for removing lead from petrol; the metal is certainly toxic, and while the worldwide trend is towards lead-free petrol Britain would be wise to follow.' It then went on to say that it believed '... decisions on issues of this kind should be taken on the basis of reliable scientific evidence, not emotional propaganda'. Associated Octel frequently quoted these last words out of context, implying that the BMJ either had no view on the issue or opposed a ban on lead in petrol. The opposite was the case, for it twice published leading articles supporting the elimination of lead from petrol.

In its print material, Associated Octel quoted a number of so-called scientists, most notably its medical officer for over 30 years, as authorities on lead and health, but failed to answer any of the four major studies on health risks that were the basis of the CLEAR campaign. In fact, it did not even refer to any of them or their authors in some of its brochures.

Associated Octel claimed to spend a fortune on 'objective research' into lead and health, but self-exposed these claims as untrue when it put a letter to workers on factory notice-boards stating that in answer to proposals for reductions of lead in petrol 'the company's activities over a wide field covering government departments, *research establishments*, contacts with MPs, etc, *to resist these proposals* have been known from time to time through our established consultative channels' (my italics). Associated Octel did its best to discover CLEAR's plans and when we were making a provincial tour it telephoned local television and radio stations seeking equal time. This, incidentally, we welcomed because these encounters inevitably were beneficial to CLEAR rather than Associated Octel.

Associated Octel also organised a series of lunches at Locketts Restaurant in London at which it sought to persuade MPs of the weakness of our case. The company even took over one of the most expensive restaurants in Strasbourg to wine and dine Euro-MPs.

All of the industries kept up the same series of charges: that our campaign was 'emotional'; that there was no evidence to link low-level lead exposure with health; and that the costs and technical difficulties would be too great.

We countered these by saying that rather than being emotional, we were presenting scientific material in a scientific context coolly and factually; we countered their charge that there was no evidence by developing a slide show for audiences and detailed print material demonstrating the studies, their methodology and results; we countered the 'cost' argument with our own survey of petrol prices in the USA. We established that on the American experience petrol prices would increase by between 1 and 2 per cent in Britain if we moved to lead-free petrol.

In April we received a breakthrough in the scientific argument in the form of two major studies, both of them supportive of our position. The first, a massive study in the USA, showed that by the time 55 per cent of the lead had been eliminated from petrol in America, blood-lead levels across the country as a whole had fallen by 37 per cent. Statistical analysis of the studies, and interpretation by experts on behalf of the Environmental Protection Agency, led to the conclusion that the key factor in the reduction in blood-lead levels was the reduction in lead in petrol. This helped to demolish the case of the industries that petrol-lead was not the main contributor to body-lead burdens. Our case in this respect was further boosted by the first results of an Italian study. This too showed a clear relationship between petrol-lead and lead in blood. We worked hard to publicise these studies and achieved a major article in *The Sunday Times* and also news stories in other publications.

It is, incidentally, worth noting that this is one of the benefits that pressure groups offer. Had CLEAR not existed, it is doubtful whether knowledge of these international studies would have ever been communicated in Britain. Assuming that the information was acquired by the British authorities at all, they would have had no incentive to publish it. The industries would not have published it. And thus it would never have been known.

With the help of contacts within the Labour Party, we were able to place before Labour's NEC a powerful document on the effects of lead in petrol, and the NEC decided unanimously to support lead-free petrol. As the Falklands crisis was breaking, this was not picked up by political writers, but once more we were able to demonstrate how a pressure group can make sure that such initiatives do not go without notice. We tipped off friends in national newspapers and widespread publicity was achieved for the Labour decision.

By now the campaign had been going for nearly four months and we came to one of the main events on our campaign calendar – our three-day international symposium on lead and health. From the start we knew we would stand or fall on our ability to give respectability to the medical and scientific case, and this was our main throw. We had raised the money – including a

£15,000 donation by a food company – to invite to Britain all of the scientists who had produced major studies on lead and health, and we now invited everyone concerned with the issue in Britain to come to a symposium to hear reports on the studies and to cross-examine the researchers. We invited representatives of the different ministries involved, all of the members of the Lawther committee, environmental health officers and the scientific media, and we advertised it widely so that representatives of the petroleum industry and Associated Octel figured in the audience as well. We set the whole symposium up to the standards that would be expected of a high-quality scientific symposium. However, we still had to overcome the possible charge that the conference was loaded in support of our case. We therefore decided to seek a chairman about whom that charge could not possibly be made. The ideal candidate was Professor Michael Rutter, perhaps the leading child psychiatrist in the world, and a member of the Lawther committee. To our surprise he accepted the invitation.

We had taken a substantial gamble. If, after hearing all the evidence, this distinguished scientist concluded there was no health hazard, it would be a major set-back and mean that all the money we had invested had been wasted. Thus we genuinely put the evidence on the line, trusting in the integrity of this respected scientist but, above all, trusting in the strength of our case. It is no exaggeration to say that when Rutter rose to his feet to summarise the conference we felt that he had it within his capacity at that moment to boost our chances of success substantially or set them back, perhaps beyond redemption. What happened is perhaps best independently described – by Geoffrey Lean in his article in *The Observer* the following Sunday:

> Last week's call [for lead-free petrol] by Professor Michael Rutter, one of the world's leading child psychiatrists, has made a strong impact. Professor Rutter is a member of the Committee most respected in Whitehall and officials have frequently pointed to his signature on the Lawther report as showing that there is no need for a ban. His statement signals that the weight of medical opinion has now moved behind a ban. This is the result of a bold gamble by CLEAR. ... It invited Professor Rutter to chair the symposium, not knowing whether he had changed his mind since signing the Lawther report, but confident that he would make up his mind on the evidence. To experts in the audience the meeting took on the atmosphere of a tribunal rather than a symposium, with Professor Rutter keenly questioning each speaker. By the end of the three-day conference most were expecting a cautious and qualified endorsement of lead-free fuel. But after a thoughtful 5,000-word review of the evidence, Professor Rutter called trenchantly and unequivocably for immediate action.

> He described the reduction announced by the Government last year as an unacceptable compromise without clear advantages and with definite disadvantages. He added 'The evidence suggests that the removal of lead from petrol would have a quite substantial effect in reducing lead pollution, and the costs are quite modest by any reasonable standard.'
>
> In passing he demolished many of the basic arguments of the Lawther Committee's report. ... His statement demolishes the entire platform on which the Government has stood. And, even worse for Ministers, it is not an isolated event. A substantial number of the Lawther Committee's members have now come to similar conclusions.
>
> The Committee has split into hard-line opponents of a ban, many of whom failed even to reply to invitations to the symposium, and others who are moved towards recommending a ban. Five of the 12 members attended the meeting.

Unfortunately, the Falklands War was now under way and even the CLEAR campaign could not compete with that for editorial space. The symposium did not get the publicity it otherwise would have done, but nevertheless it had been a major set-back for all of our opponents. We finally took a break and breather for the summer, more than content that we had won every battle in our war so far and were immeasurably strengthened by the experience.

Over the summer, we considered what we had achieved. First, from the small number of organisations declared as supporters at the beginning, we had experienced almost a landslide of support, so that in my book *The Lead Scandal* I was able to show the line-up after six months as follows:

Supporting lead in petrol
DoE Minister Giles Shaw and his civil servants
Health Minister Kenneth Clarke and his civil servants
Transport Minister Lynda Chalker and her civil servants
The petroleum industry
The car manufacturers
The lead industry
Associated Octel

Calling for a ban on lead in petrol
The Labour Party
The Liberal Party
The Social Democratic Party
The Scottish National Party

The Ecology Party
Over 100 local authorities
The National Consumer Council
The Consumers' Association
The National Society for Clean Air
The Institution of Environmental Health Officers
The Trades Union Congress (representing 11 million trade unionists)
The National Association of Health Authorities
The National Association of Head Teachers
The Inner London Education Authority
The National Association of Youth Clubs
The National Association of Women's Clubs
The Advisory Centre for Education
The Association of Directors of Social Services
The Association of Neighbourhood Councils
CALIP
The Association of Community Health Councils for England and Wales
The Cleaner London Campaign
The Conservation Society
Friends of the Earth
The Health Visitors Association
The London Amenity and Transport Association
The Pedestrians Association
The Spastics Society
Transport 2000
The National Children's Centre
The Rambler's Association
The West Indian Standing Conference
200 Members of Parliament
Over 50 members of the House of Lords
60% of GPs (*Doctor* magazine poll)
90% of British public (MORI poll)
The Times
The Observer
Guardian
London *Evening Standard*
Doctor magazine
World Medicine
New Scientist
British Medical Journal

Second, all of the medical and scientific evidence that had emerged since the launch had been supportive of our case, and we had now drawn to our side such scientists as Rutter and thus achieved genuine medical and scientific respectability.

Third, we had shown that this relatively narrow issue could remain in the forefront of attention month after month, provided one had sufficient ideas for action and worked hard enough to do it.

We were now a highly respectable cause, both in terms of acceptance of our argument and in terms of our status, and the next step was to return with vigour in the autumn and surprise both ministers and the industries with our stamina on the issue – our ability to keep them on the defensive and to keep hitting until eventually they simply could not withstand the pressure. But how?

First, we decided on a number of fresh studies. We sent a detailed questionnaire on local authority monitoring practice to all environmental health officers. Second, we sent a van, manned by FoE pollution consultant Brian Price and an assistant, to schools in cities around the country to collect dust samples from playgrounds and pavements. This achieved widespread publicity wherever it went, while at the same time providing evidence of the relationship between lead emitted from car exhausts and lead in the vicinity of school buildings. Third, we raised the money from a trust to finance a study of lead in vegetables grown in allotments and gardens in London. The aim of the experience was to see whether the lead levels in vegetables in areas of higher traffic density was higher than the lead levels in outer suburbs.

Second, we planned a major assault on the party conferences. Fringe meetings were fixed for each, and material was dispersed widely. As a member of the Liberal Party, I was able to move a resolution at the assembly, with full television coverage and widespread publicity the following day. We launched our autumn campaign with a press conference attended by Gerald Kaufman, Shadow Cabinet Environmental spokesman, who irrevocably committed Labour to a ban on lead. At the same press conference we unveiled our survey of local authorities showing that 85 per cent of those that had taken a policy decision on lead in petrol supported the drive to have it eliminated. We *also* published the results of our survey into monitoring.

About the same time Associated Octel demonstrated their extraordinary capacity to score own goals. They spent a small fortune on full-page ads in all of the major national newspapers presenting their case under the absurd heading 'The Health and Wealth of the Nation . This proved totally counterproductive. First, it was so hopelessly inaccurate that it actually led to condemnation by the Advertising Standards Authority, who upheld a considerable number of public complaints. Second, I was able to write to newspapers such as *The Observer* and *The Sunday Times* and have letters published pointing out the errors and putting our alternative case. Third, it actually contributed to drawing widespread attention to the issue without achieving any credibility for Associated Octel. They had effectively spent over £100,000 giving us new issue-visibility and momentum that we possibly could not have achieved without them. With enemies like this, we thought, who needed friends?

We had worked to make sure that the TUC would pass a resolution for lead-free petrol and this also achieved widespread publicity.

Undoubtedly the autumn campaign came as a blow to the petroleum industry and the car manufacturing industry, who had hoped that as a result of the summer break we had lost momentum. I have been reliably told that the petroleum industry, who after all are the owners of Associated Octel, were furious at the latter's clumsy advertising campaign. We still, however, had one or two moves up our sleeve for the autumn, for we had been working hard to persuade the consumer bodies to launch a European campaign. Earlier in the year I had travelled to Brussels and met Tony Venables, of BEUC (European Bureau of Consumer Unions) and Hubert David, then director of the European Environmental Bureau, and presented them with the evidence of harm caused by lead in petrol and the need for action. For the first time ever, these two organisations decided to launch a joint campaign across the whole of Europe on the issue, and I travelled to Brussels several times to help plan this campaign. It was decided to launch it in all the major European capitals on the same day, and I attended the main launch in Brussels, whilst one of the CLEAR committee members went to the London launch. This once more achieved considerable publicity in Britain.

So came Christmas, and the New Year, and the campaign was one year old. We were aware that the Royal Commission on Environmental Pollution had decided to study the issue. This concerned us, because at the least three members of the commission had always been on the opposite side in the scientific debate. Furthermore, the commission had indicated that they would not reopen the question of health damage explored by the Lawther committee. We decided, therefore, that there was a risk of a whitewash and that this should be anticipated in two ways: first, we should make clear in advance our concern about the Royal Commission so that if its conclusions were unsatisfactory, we could not be said to have condemned them after the event simply because they did not share our view; second, we would mount a sufficiently powerful campaign prior to publication of its report to balance any impact that a negative report might make.

Given the ultimate conclusions of the Royal Commission, we clearly did it an injustice, although it has to be said that we have every reason to believe that the three people whom we distrusted were in fact the main advocates of an alternative commission conclusion. I believe our tactics were correct, with one exception. In my book *The Lead Scandal,* due to be published shortly before the Royal Commission reported, I perhaps overstated our justification for anticipating a whitewash. (At our press conference after the publication of the Royal Commission report, in the presence of its chairman, I made a point of saying how pleased I was to be able to admit I had been in error.)

The proceedings of our 1982 symposium were being published in March 1983 and I met Professor Rutter, who had co-edited the proceedings with Robin Russell Jones, to discuss his position in the light of his conclusions at the symposium. He said he felt able to make a further intervention on the issue, provided it was in a suitably scientific setting, and we decided to stage a special lecture by him to mark the publication of the book. Rutter on that occasion pointedly, although not by name, criticised the overstating of the health damage by Derek Bryce-Smith, but also made clear that this criticism did not in his view extend to CLEAR. He went on to argue even more forcibly that the evidence justified the elimination of lead from petrol.

Roger Ratcliffe of *The Sunday Times,* another journalist with a splendid record on this particular issue, then persuaded Dr Richard Lansdown, another controversial scientist concerned with the issue, to say that he felt the evidence now justified action. *The Sunday Times* made the story of the conversion of Rutter and Lansdown their front page lead on 6 March. The following day *The Times* published a letter signed by a number of leading politicians, scientists, trade union leaders and general secretaries of supporting organisations, calling for action.

However, we were now about to play the two cards provided by the research we had commissioned six months earlier. The first was the result of our survey of lead in dust outside schools all over the country. The levels were sufficiently high to achieve considerable national publicity, and even more at local level. Many local newspapers made it their front-page headlines. The result was fresh uproar. A few days later we held a press conference to publish the result of the investigation into lead in vegetables by Welsh scientist Dr Brian Davies. He had found that 40 per cent of land in inner London and 20 per cent in outer London was unsuitable for growing vegetables. We fielded at the same press conference the senior medical consultant for the Automobile Association, Dr James Bevan, who underlined the health risk. The lead-in-vegetables study caused another uproar. It was the front-page lead in London's *Evening Standard.*

There is no question that by this time it had become clear to senior people in the Conservative administration that they were faced with a campaign of pressure they were unable to combat. The industries had virtually conceded defeat, and it was being acknowledged that whereas they could have withstood the scientific case that had been accumulated if it had not been reinforced by a pressure group, and they could have survived the activities of a pressure group if not supported by scientific evidence, the combination was unbeatable.

Now things began to move swiftly. First, the Royal Commission concluded that it should recommend the elimination of lead from petrol, and this was reported to Tom King, by then Secretary of State, and Giles Shaw, the junior minister who had from the start handled the affair so badly from the government's point of view. At the same time, influential people close to the Prime Minister were suggesting to her that with an election pending it was foolish to be so isolated on the wrong side of an argument about the health of children. There is little question that Downing Street indicated to Tom King that a face-saving solution would be helpful, and that Tom King seized upon the Royal Commission report for that solution.

It is noteworthy that the previous report by the Royal Commission on Environmental Pollution on air pollution had to wait seven years for a governmental response, and the response was basically negative. Thus a Royal Commission report on its own was hardly likely to influence the government; what made the difference was that the government was actually looking for a way out of the corner into which Giles Shaw and some civil servants had backed it.

Geoffrey Lean of *The Observer* had been diligently exploring the activities of the Royal Commission and on 3 April reported that their findings, to be published on 18 April, would in fact come down on the side of CLEAR. By then the decision had probably been taken at ministerial level to move to lead-free petrol and from CLEAR's point of view it was not a day too soon because the campaign was about to face its first set-back. It had its origins in research commissioned two years previously on the links between low-level lead exposure and health. Unfortunately the research had been given to scientists who were members of the Lawther committee, or who were part of a group who had publicly consistently defined the strength of the evidence on the issue. CLEAR had consistently warned for over a year that this research would have no standing in the campaign's eyes. In fact it did identify an IQ deficit in children with higher lead levels, but it attempted to show that there were other probable reasons, such as social class, for this.

The DoE, still at civil service level fighting their battle with CLEAR, took the unusual step of releasing their version of the evidence plus their interpretation of it. Once more the value of a pressure group was made apparent because when CLEAR was telephoned by the newspapers, we were able to react quickly by condemning the way the material was being released to create the impression that the reports wholly supported the DoE view when they did not. As a result, the government was angered to find the headlines 'Government delivers verdict without releasing studies' in the *Guardian* and 'Lead reports cause fury' in the *Birmingham Post* with the stories largely dominated by our protest about the way the research was being manipulated by DoE public relations people.

The fact that at this point the already-taken ministerial decision to move to lead-free petrol was restricted to Downing Street and Tom King was reflected in the fact that on 9 April in the House of Commons Lynda Chalker, junior Transport Minister, was still arguing that exhaust filters were the best way to move to lead-free petrol. However, during the weekend of 16–17 April the government moved to make it clear that they were going to accept the Royal Commission's recommendations the following Monday. The fact that Mrs Thatcher was now personally involved was demonstrated by the breadth of the leaks and references such as that in the *Mail on Sunday* that 'the decision by Mrs Thatcher and other Ministers effectively steals some of Labour's political clothes', and in the *News of the World*, 'Premier Margaret Thatcher has decided to respond swiftly to a Royal Commission report'.

At 2.30 pm on Monday, 18 April, Professor Richard Southwood, chairman of the Royal Commission on Environmental Pollution, duly presented his report at a press conference and called for the elimination of lead from petrol. I was in the Strangers Gallery in the House of Commons at 3.30 pm that afternoon to hear Tom King accept that recommendation and announce that the government would press for a European-wide ban on lead in petrol. 'Rout of stout party: environmental ministers seen heading for the policy hills with the Royal Commission on Environmental Pollution and Clear – The Campaign for Lead-free Air – in full pursuit,' said the Guardian in a leader the following day. It was, said *The Times* in a leader, 'Good Riddance to Lead'.

We held our own press conference after Tom King, calling for the introduction of a definite date and saying that if there were delays in Europe, Britain should act unilaterally. But the battle on the principle was over. Of course, we did not then have lead-free petrol, and CLEAR remained in being to fight for a definite and early date to persuade other European countries to move to lead-free petrol as well and to make sure that there was no sell-out. (There wasn't. By 1993 half the petrol sold in the UK was lead-free.) But the aim of the exercise was *a decision* – a decision by ministers who did not want to take that decision, a decision in the face of Whitehall opposition, a decision in the face of the expenditure of vast resources by huge industries, a decision that was a reversal of an earlier governmental decision two years earlier.

Was it because of the election? Perhaps that helped, but lead-free petrol would have been irrelevant to the election if CLEAR had not politicised the issue to the point where it was a factor. The Royal Commission's report was highly influential, but the Royal Commission only decided to look at the lead issue as a result of the CLEAR campaign and earlier Royal Commission reports had to wait between two and seven years before notice was taken of them. Full credit had to be given to those in the Conservation Society and others who had worked on the issue before May 1981, but the fact is that the end result of their efforts had been a decision to reduce only to 0.15 grams per litre. CLEAR was, therefore, entitled to claim the decision as a result of its campaign; as a demonstration of the role and value of pressure groups when our institutions fail; and as reassurance that if people unite, contribute their money and their skills and their energies, and pursue their cause professionally with a sense of perspective and with perseverance, they can triumph over considerable odds in protecting their interests.

Looking back over those 15 months one can see there were a number of crucial moments:

- First, the publication of the Yellowlees letter in the early days added enormous authority to our case that there was a health hazard.
- Second, the opinion poll with its extraordinary show of support entitled CLEAR to say that it spoke for a huge constituency.
- Third, the international symposium and the conversion of Professor Michael Rutter was a crucial psychological blow.
- Fourth, the initiatives CLEAR took to dramatise the problem – the lead in dust survey outside schools, the lead in vegetables study and so on – achieved colossal publicity and aroused enormous support.

Of all the activities we undertook, the tremendous effort we made to build up support from organisations, politicians and local authorities was perhaps the most valuable. However, I believe there are lessons for others in the way we determined realistic objectives, in the quality of our research linked to our determination to project our case with real authority, and in the way we refused to be diverted from our own campaign plan and our own battleground to that of our opponents.

The other side, particularly the industries, have their own version of events. Above all, they argued and would still argue that we exaggerated the health case and deliberately frightened people for no reason. It is, of course, true that we aroused concern all over the country about the health risk. But that was our task. It was precisely because the authorities refused to acknowledge it that we had to do this. I do not believe that people should be denied the knowledge of research and studies that indicate health problems. The people of Britain are adult and mature enough to consider the facts objectively and reach their own conclusions. Their instinctive human response was that they did not care whether the evidence was conclusive or not, for they could see that there were sufficient organisations and people of substance who were prepared to state that it was a risk, and they wanted action on the basis of risk. Not for them conclusive proof, which would have been achievable only by what would in effect have been experiment with their children.

I believe a number of other lessons can be learned from this campaign. The authorities have to learn that people expect higher priority for environmental protection – that they rate the health of their children much more highly than the performance of their cars or the price of petrol. The industries have to learn that instead of trying to withstand the increasing concern for environmental protection, they would do far better to respond positively to it, for if they do not they will end up being forced to act – often more expensively than if they had acted voluntarily. And hopefully the parents of this country have learned that when the democratic process fails them, when their institutions fail to respond, there is still hope – hope in the alternative ways of becoming involved, in voluntary organisations, charities and pressure groups with a legitimate role in the democratic process and offering another way to exercise power.

6 Case history: Parents against Tobacco

At the end of 1989 Britain's Chief Medical Officer of Health confirmed that cigarette smoking was 'by far the most important single cause of ill-health and premature death, and hence of expenditure on health services'. This reflected a World Health Organization survey revealing that 'some 50,000 studies have irrefutably established the link between tobacco and disease'.

Anti-smoking groups approached Citizen Action, the campaigning group I directed with the support of my friend Godfrey Bradman, and asked if we could contribute to the preventive health cause. In particular they asked whether we could help tackle the problem of illegal sales of cigarettes to children.

No one believed that making it more difficult for children to buy cigarettes would in itself stop the more determined ones from getting them or smoking them ... it was not *the* answer to the problem, but it was a prerequisite for solving it. Apart from making sense in itself, it would add credibility to laws restricting the sale of cigarettes to children and it would add credibility to parental warnings about the dangers of smoking, for why should children believe smoking was really damaging if they could easily purchase cigarettes from the nearest shop?

In late 1989 we contributed to a series of surveys of 418 shops showing that, despite laws going back to 1904 forbidding the sale of cigarettes to children below the age of 16, 224 shops – more than half – sold cigarettes to children as young as 12. It was clear that retailers were ignoring the law.

Further research showed that this contempt for the law was made more serious by confusion among the local authorities and the police over who was responsible for enforcement.

That's why we decided to launch a campaign with one over-riding aim: to get the law changed in order to make it more effective.

Our objectives included:

1 making it mandatory for local authorities to maintain surveillance over the problem and to prosecute offenders;
2 increasing the fines to make them a genuine deterrent;
3 making it illegal for traders to break open packs and sell single cigarettes to anyone;
4 tightening up control of vending machine sales;
5 making shops display effective warning notices about the illegality of selling cigarettes to children.

The campaign succeeded. Its proposed legislation – not seriously weakened by some minor compromises – is now the law of the land.

This is the story of that campaign.

FOCUS ON PARENTS

Why did we make it *parents* against tobacco?

First, we wanted to free this particular campaign from the controversies over individual freedom and the right of adults to tell other adults what they should do. That way, we wrong-footed the tobacco companies and their mouthpiece organisations, who from the start found it extremely difficult to cope with PaT.

Second, we believed that an appeal from parents for help in keeping their children from smoking had a special legitimacy that would be difficult for politicians to ignore. This proved to be the case.

Third, by inviting well-known personalities to support the campaign as *parents* concerned about their *own children*, we were able to break down the inevitable resistance from busy and overstressed people to get involved in 'yet another cause'.

At the launch we identified four differences between our campaign and others:

1 PaT would not be directed at adult smokers.
2 Our legitimacy would come from the rights of parents to protect their children.
3 We would not seek official funding.

4 Our attack would be directly aimed at the industry – the people we described as tobacco traffickers.

We decided to involve parents at two levels:

- At national level, we would put together an organisation of 100 famous parents, some of whom could give significant time to the campaign, and some of whom would give their name and perhaps make one or two appearances.
- At local level, we would inspire PaT groups – or at least effective local PaT co-ordinators – to reflect in their own communities what we were doing and saying nationally.

When the campaign was launched we were able to produce stars from the cinema and television, the arts, sport, politics, journalism and medical science. This made a considerable impact.

COALITION ACTIVITY

We also got together more than 50 local groups or co-ordinators who were able to achieve considerable publicity at local level and, before the campaign was launched, we put together an impressive coalition of every kind of voluntary national organisation likely to be concerned about smoking: health care and research bodies, women's and mothers' institutions and, of course, those concerned with children and education. In the end, more than 60 respected national organisations put their names and weight behind PaT.

We circulated all members of the House of Commons and got together a list of more than 200 political supporters of all political parties.

We took the idea to top preventive health organisations, ranging from Europe against Cancer in Brussels to the Health Education Authority and Richard Branson's Healthcare Foundation – even the Readers' Digest Trust. They all liked it and were prepared to fund it generously. On the quality of the idea alone, before the campaign was launched we raised the UK equivalent of over half a million dollars.

THE LAUNCH

We employed someone with legal training to research every aspect of the problem and how it was being tackled in other countries. We carried out our own surveys of illegal sales, and put together an impressive folio of print material based on all our research. In January 1990 we launched the campaign at a major press conference in London. It featured such publicity-attracting people as the Duke of Gloucester, Richard Branson, Anita Roddick, Lynne Faulds Wood, Clare Rayner and England rugby star Richard Hill.

The press conference was packed, not only with newspaper journalists and radio and television crews, but also with representatives of the supporting organisations and the 100 parents.

The combination of the idea, the personalities and the kind of subject the media love – bad retailers selling killer products to innocent children – guaranteed huge coverage.

Soon leaders of all political parties – including the Prime Minister, Mrs Thatcher – had indicated support. Other famous people got in touch and said they would like to help too.

Already we felt we had won the first round, namely to get the problem of illegal sales acknowledged and to get broad support for action. What we now had to do was turn this support into effective, sustained pressure for legislative action.

PRIVATE MEMBER'S BILL

As we have described earlier in this book (see pages 131 to 160), while it is the government of the day which initiates most legislation, there is one particular opportunity for outsiders to get legislation enacted. It is called the private member's bill.

Each year there is a ballot which all back-bench MPs enter. The top six names drawn in the ballot have a reasonable chance of sufficient parliamentary time to get a new piece of legislation through parliament – provided, of course, that the governing party doesn't vote it down using its parliamentary majority, and that the measure can otherwise gain sufficient all-party support to prevail over those who may oppose it.

We drafted a bill to tighten up the law on the sale of cigarettes to children under 16 and began to lean on our 200 back-bench MP supporters to commit themselves to introducing it if they came in the top six in the ballot. Apart from lobbying at Westminster, we decided to apply pressure at grassroots constituency level with our Back the Bill campaign.

THE PAT BUS

We did this mainly with our PaT roadshow ... our own Back the Bill double-decker bus, painted white with the PaT logo and campaign message all over it. This toured 137 towns. At each stop people had the chance to fill in a postcard to their MP and post it in our own post-box. More than 5,000 cards were sent.

Everywhere the bus went it was noticed. It was covered by 150 local newspapers, 38 radio stations and nine local television stations. Local mayors and other celebrities came to meet it. DJs from radio stations and actors appearing in local theatres were invited to have their pictures taken, surrounded by local children, with the bus.

We also took the bus to Westminster and MPs flocked to have their picture taken at the wheel; we then sent the pictures to their local newspapers: good PR for the MP and for PaT.

This bus proved a huge success – as a collector of postcards, as a publicity-getter, and also as a focal point for activity by local PaT groups and others campaigning on health issues.

LOCAL AUTHORITIES

We also worked to get local authorities to apply pressure on national authorities and got more than 320 of Britain's local district, city and county councils to pass resolutions supporting PaT.

We did this by circulating a model resolution to all councils. This resolution not only gave support to PaT but caused councils to take immediate action – such as banning tobacco advertising on council-owned land, which many councils did. And it raised a surprising amount of money.

Many local authorities really got the bit between their teeth and began to monitor illegal cigarette sales without waiting to see if we could change the law. The number of local council surveys soared. The number of prosecutions increased.

From local authorities the pressure on MPs grew.

SCHOOLS

We now turned our attention to schools. We wanted to involve them for two reasons:

- First, we wanted children to play a part in the campaign too.
- Second, we knew school activity would impact on local media and on parents.

So we launched our schools competition.

Apple Computers, who were anxious to raise their profile in the education world, were persuaded to donate $15,000-worth of computer equipment to the main prizewinning school. We gave cash prizes for winners in other categories.

The aim was to find Britain's top smoke-free school ... the one with the most imaginative, wide-ranging and effective anti-smoking programme involving students, teachers and parents. The other categories included:

- PaT's young reporter;
- PaT's young designer;
- PaT's sports personality interview of the year;
- PaT's rap of the year.

Details were mailed to all schools and the competition was endorsed by the Secretary of State for Education. The prizes were presented at an end-of-the-year ceremony in London, by the Duke of Gloucester.

The competition did much to mobilise schools behind the anti-smoking message while getting the additional momentum we wanted for our campaign.

PAT UNITED

Nor did our campaign in schools stop there.

We were anxious to counter the way the tobacco industry uses glamorous images, especially sporting and leisure pursuit images, to sell cigarettes. We persuaded some of Britain's top sports stars to pose in PaT sweat-shirts to endorse the campaign, and to each spend a day or two in visiting schools to give master classes in their sport and speak to the school assembly about the way smoking ruins fitness and sporting ability.

We called our team 'PaT United' and it was launched at a media photo opportunity at a London school. Members included a number of Olympic champions; the captains of England's cricket and soccer teams, Graham Gooch and Gary Lineker; rubgy stars; a former world boxing champion; and the champion steeplechase jockey. One member, Sally Gunnell, subsequently became Olympic and world champion and recordholder in the 400 metres hurdles. Our team 'captain' was Olympic javelin champion Tessa Sanderson.

PaT on the Back

So we had mobilised parents, organisations, stars, politicians, local councils and schools. One group remained: the retailers themselves.

We decided to encourage the responsible retailers and further highlight the problem by publicising and rewarding shopkeepers who refused to sell cigarettes to children. We called it our 'PaT on the Back' scheme.

Local groups gave PaT on the Back certificates to tried and tested local shops and arranged press publicity for the awards. In addition we brought retailers from all over the country to London for a national awards ceremony hosted by Richard Branson of Virgin Airlines.

All these activities were organised by a young, enthusiastic team working on temporary contracts for low pay. Each had responsibility for one of the projects – the PaT bus, schools competition, the PaT United team, PaTon the back and so on.

Progressing the Campaign

By the autumn of 1990, Jane Dunmore, who ran the political side of the campaign, had secured firm promises from MPs of all parties that if they came high in the ballot they would introduce a bill. We were also hopeful that many more would respond favourably.

We had the industry on the run, and we had gained enormous goodwill behind our drive for legislative change.

On the MPs' ballot day in November we recruited the help of three MPs – one from each of the main parties – took over a room in the Palace of Westminster with our full team equipped with mobile phones and information kits and waited for the ballot. As each name was called we were ready to set off to find the MP, knowing we were 'competing' with about 50 other lobbyists with other cherished issues to pursue.

Well, every campaign needs a bit of luck, and we got it. The number 1 in the ballot, Labour MP Andrew Faulds, was on our list of supporters. I raced through the palace to his office and found him dictating letters to his secretary. At first he was reluctant to commit himself. But I knew we had to get commitment to the bill before others could get to him and applied every bit of pressure I could – including the fact that a television crew was waiting outside to give immediate publicity to whoever took on the bill. Faulds folded. We went straight out and announced that he would introduce the bill. We had got our MP – we were on our way.

We had a head start over other pressure groups competing for parliamentary time because we had built up public enthusiasm for the measure we proposed, we had a fully drafted bill, and we had an experienced team to give the MP all the professional back-up required. But that was still only the start. We had to build up a parliamentary coalition behind the bill and steer it through various readings, especially the detailed committee-stage discussions. We had to stop the government from weakening it drastically – as they were clearly inclined to do under pressure from the tobacco lobbyists, get it past the House of Lords, and finally see it working as the law of the land.

It was a long and tough process, involving many hours of negotiations with at least four different government departments. Jane had discussions with ministers at the Home Office, the health and environment departments and the Department of Trade and Industry over a period of months, and she had many late-night drafting sessions going through clauses line by line with officials before each parliamentary sitting on the bill.

THE BILL BECOMES LAW

Eventually we won the battle. The Children and Young Persons (Protection from Tobacco) Act became law in June 1991.

Even then the fight was not over. While the main part of the organisation closed down after the first crucial year of building up the campaign on a broad front, Jane was kept hard at it ensuring that the advice sent by the national authorities to local authorities was strong and accurate, and that the various measures in the Act were adopted and put into effect.

What does the Act do?

- It increases the maximum fine for the illegal sale of cigarettes six-fold.
- It extends controls to vending machines.
- It puts the responsibility for monitoring and enforcing the law clearly on the shoulders of local authorities.
- It prohibits the sale of single cigarettes.
- It requires a warning about the illegality of sales to children to be published on cigarette packets and in stores.

In addition, although the UK government is still standing out against a regulatory ban on print and poster tobacco advertising, we were influential in securing changes to the voluntary tobacco advertising agreement. Shopfront advertising, while not banned altogether, will be cut by 50 per cent, with shops near schools targeted first.

Is the problem of children smoking solved?

Of course not.

But when the legislation is widely implemented (and PaT continues to campaign on that) and becomes fully effective, the law will be much better known, it will be much more dangerous for retailers to sell tobacco illegally, and it will be clearer to children that parents really believe the message that cigarettes are bad news.

What led to the campaign's success?

- Good planning.
- A terrific team of young organisers, each responsible for one activity.
- Effective fund-raising, especially in persuading major institutions such as the Health Education Authority, Richard Branson's Healthcare Foundation and the Europe against Cancer Campaign to donate.
- The recruitment of well-known names (promising them the campaign would only last a year helped enormously).
- Good ideas – PaT United and Pat on the Back especially.

But above all, success came from a good case well argued with determination and the maximum use of personalities and other organisations. It was a classic single-issue coalition campaign.

7 Case history: Crossrail

BACKGROUND

Crossrail is planned as a major rail project intended to create a direct fast east–west rail link across London. Estimated to cost about £2 billion, it's a joint venture between British Rail and London Underground and has considerable business and community support. Its promoters claim it will have many benefits, not least relieving traffic congestion, providing better access, diverting many journeys from road to rail and providing a direct rail route from the City to Heathrow.

All was going well until the spring of 1993 when the second reading of the Crossrail private bill was postponed at the Treasury's insistence.

The Department of Transport protested strongly, the Prime Minister became involved and from the subsequent negotiations emerged the Chancellor's Budget Day compromise that the government remained 'committed to securing for London the benefits that Crossrail will bring' but that it now believed it should proceed as a joint venture with the private sector. He said: 'The present proposals for Crossrail will therefore be re-examined ... our aim will be to maximise the participation and financial involvement of the private sector and to secure the best value for money for the taxpayer.'

The Treasury then commissioned Bechtel and Warburg to reassess the project's viability and value, establish whether savings can be made and advise on whether it was likely to attract private finance. The findings were to be with the Treasury in the first week of May. It was reliably reported that they would be generally positive, finding the scheme to be well considered and capable of attracting private sector funding.

The Treasury would then have to decide whether, despite the expected findings, it still wished to stop the project. There were grounds for believing that it would if it could. If the Treasury persuaded the Cabinet to stop Crossrail, government managers would have three options:

1 Parliamentary action to defeat it at second reading. This was unlikely. It would be politically clumsy and unpredictable.

2 An open government decision to kill it once and for all on the grounds that it was too heavy a burden on the exchequer. This would be accompanied by a refusal to authorise parliamentary time.

3 An unofficial exercise in government sabotage. If managers decided on this course, they would act procedurally – by delaying the second reading and the committee stage so that inadequate progress was made before the summer recess.

The real concern was that any delay would have been seriously damaging; from the autumn the existing private bill procedure would no longer have been available. The untested replacement procedure was likely to be complex and protracted and destructive for Crossrail, possibly terminally so.

So it was vital that either:

1 the Treasury was discouraged from attempting to persuade the government to abandon Crossrail; or

2 if the Treasury did attempt to do so, that the government was persuaded to overrule it; and that the government was further persuaded to assist the second reading and committee stage to proceed as soon as possible.

It was in those circumstances, and working with other key organisations, that the organisation London First undertook to orchestrate a campaign to encourage the government to press ahead with Crossrail and the second reading. To do this it set out to develop a coalition of concerned organisations and it employed the services of the public affairs unit of Burson-Marsteller to undertake day-by-day activities management.

Because I believe there is a lot to learn from the relationship between planning and execution of this campaign, I will first of all outline the plan in detail and then describe what actually happened.

THE PLAN

The objective

The immediate objective was:

> To ensure the bill had a second reading and began its committee stage as soon as possible.

The strategy

The strategy was to:

1. Persuade the government that Crossrail continued to make *economic* sense – that it was a viable and valuable project. (The chances of success would be considerably enhanced if the Bechtel and Warburg reports were as positive as anticipated.)
2. Persuade the government that it made *political* sense, by demonstrating that it was widely and strongly supported by all those constituencies (in the widest sense) that the government needed to be sensitive to.

A few points about the tone of the campaign follow. It was decided that:

- It would not be the voice of just the public transport 'industry' – or of the City. It would seek to espouse the causes of both the economy generally and the quality of life of London and the south east.
- It would be forceful but not strident ... providing leadership and representation on the basis of responsible, well-researched, well-argued positions.
- Its arguments would be based mainly (although not totally) on economic and far-sighted regional developmental considerations, and would promote the project as the centrepiece of a required package of transport initiatives.
- Its key spokespeople would be drawn from those people the target audience – government itself – respected.

In other words, it would be a campaign of *substance* both in terms of breadth of support and strength of argument.

The targets

The specific nature of the objective and the lack of time at our disposal meant that we had to target directly the major governmental decision-makers – the Prime Minister (who could be the key player), the Chancellor and his fellow Treasury ministers, the Department of Transport and the Cabinet generally.

MPs were relevant, mainly in so much as they can positively influence the above.

The Prime Minister

He would:

- Be made aware of, and accountable to the strength of, feeling among traditional government supporters – business and industry, the City, MPs and local authorities in London and the south east – but also be made sensitive to the widespread general support for Crossrail.
- Be well briefed on the positive economic and other arguments for Crossrail – especially by use of the (hopefully) positive findings of Bechtel and Warburg.
- Be persuaded that this would be seen as *his* decision ... that he would be meeting part of his historic responsibility to help the nation's capital prepare itself for the twenty-first century. (He in particular had to be persuaded that cancelling Crossrail would send out all the wrong signals to the rest of Europe and the international community.)
- Be persuaded that private funders were unlikely to emerge until after second reading.

The Cabinet

The Cabinet too would:

- be made aware of the support for Crossrail;
- be properly briefed on the economic and other practical aspects of the case.

Allies needed to be identified and encouraged. Attention would be paid to the Cabinet subcommittee for London and its chairman, Michael Howard.

The Treasury

The Treasury would:

- Be shown that Crossrail was not just an obsession of British Rail and London Underground but was widely supported, and that abandoning it would be politically damaging for the government.
- Be made to see Crossrail in the widest possible context – as essential for the well-being of the nation's capital and ultimately the economy.
- Be persuaded that abandoning the project would cast a dark shadow over the whole 'private sector participation' policy.

- Be persuaded that there would be private funders but that they wouldn't emerge at this stage.
- It might be possible to demonstrate, too, that there would be an up-side for the Treasury in the form of additional taxes and reduced welfare payments.

But above all it had to be persuaded that *it couldn't win*; that there was too much political and public momentum behind the project.

The Department of Transport

Its backbone had to be stiffened. It had to be encouraged and made to feel that if it defended Crossrail it would be enthusiastically supported. It had to be persuaded to fight.

Parliamentarians

They – especially those in the south east and those representing constituencies affected by the project – would be persuaded to defend Crossrail strongly and, as they didn't have a say in the key decision (on the second reading), to *lobby for it*.

Particular attention would be paid to relevant parliamentary committees and their members, most significantly the House of Commons select committee on transport and its chairman, Robert Adley.

Campaigning priorities

Given the time factor, we decided to prioritise the campaign around only three activities:

- heavyweight and intensive lobbying;
- media publicity;
- co-ordinated and widespread expressions of support ... what we described as 'the coalition campaign'.

The lobbying campaign

Targets:

- the Prime Minister;
- the Treasury (Lamont, Portillo, Dorrell);
- the Cabinet (and the Cabinet subcommittee for London);

- the Department of Transport;
- parliamentarians (and the select committee on transport).

The *Prime Minister* would:

a) Receive a well-argued, detailed letter from a group of major figures, as well as supporting letters and submissions from other major 'players'. He must be impressed by both the quantity and quality of support for Crossrail.

b) Be requested to meet a deputation of major figures, who in turn should request him personally to see and hear a presentation of the facts.

c) Face questions at Prime Minister's question time.

d) Be requested to meet a deputation of sympathetic MPs from the south east.

The *Chancellor* would:

a) Receive a well-argued, detailed letter from a relevant set of major figures, backed up by others from individuals and organisations, all putting heavy emphasis on the economic arguments.

b) Be requested to hear personally the full case for Crossrail.

c) Be forced to take into account and respond properly to the Bechtel and Warburg reports.

d) *If they existed*, be confronted with potential private investors.

e) Be requested to meet a deputation of MPs.

Cabinet members would be individually lobbied and provided with briefings.

Meetings would take place with *Department of Transport* ministers and political advisers, and evidence would be produced of the support they have and the campaign we will be mounting. They would be offered every encouragement.

A meeting would be arranged with the chairman of the *Cabinet subcommittee for London*.

MPs would need to be lobbied and then those who were identified as supporters would themselves be used as lobbyists. Starting points would be MPs whose constituents were affected, London and south-east MPs generally, and those with transport interests, notably members of the select committee on transport.

Early decisions would be taken on:

- *what* we wanted to say,
- *to whom*,
- *when*,
- *by whom*.

In addition to the above, all the 'targets' would be exposed to media coverage, letters from a wide variety of individuals and organisations and other direct approaches.

We recognised that in all lobbying it was crucial that we use all the material at our disposal, including the Bechtel and Warburg reports and the work of the London First transport working group. It would be necessary to use these ahead of completion or publication because of the time factor.

The media campaign

The media campaign would be directed at the above 'targets' and intended to strengthen the impression that Crossrail was a politically advantageous project.

As a focal point for the campaign we would have a major press conference in London at which major names from each sector of our coalition declared their support and at which the arguments would be fully made. Around this press conference we would seek to develop considerable publicity by advance briefings and distribution of material.

An early meeting should be arranged with the editorial management of the *Evening Standard* to get its full and day-by-day campaigning support.

All transport, political and other relevant correspondents on national newspapers would be fully briefed, and in addition our contacts would be used to persuade editors to give Crossrail personal support. The media campaign would need to be sustained throughout the three or four weeks of the campaign by the unveiling of new supporters, reporters of activities and other means.

However, we realised that, whatever else it needed, the media campaign needed to have focus to ensure that it impacted on the targets of the campaign and reinforced the lobbying and coalition activity.

The coalition activity

Each member organisation of the coalition would be asked to commit itself to:

- Naming a senior representative who for the short period of this campaign had the authority to give time and to help obtain organisational resources in support of the campaign.
- Use its lobbying influence – co-ordinated by the lobbying meeting referred to above.
- Join in and support all campaigning activities and events, including deputations, letter-writing, briefings for MPs, assistance with media and so on.

The coalition co-ordinator would be in constant touch, co-ordinating all that was happening, recruiting further help and encouraging further activity.

The message

Clearly the detailed messages had to be related to the lobbying approach indicated early and would be essentially based on the *economic* and *capital city and regional developmental* arguments.

However, there were other messages that needed to be transmitted if we were to build up as broad a base of support as possible. Subsidiary messages would include:

Crossrail will be:

a) Good news for Londoners and the region generally (enhanced quality of life) and commuters because it means …

   - faster and easier journeys into and across London
   - reduced passenger congestion
   - better central area stations
   - more comfortable travel in better-designed and more spacious trains.

b) Good news for the capital city because it will enter the twenty-first century with a transport system designed to help it maintain its status as a (if not *the*) top European city. (Paris has already completed three cross-city lines and has two more in prospect.)

c) Good news for motorists because it will reduce congestion on the roads.

d) Good news environmentally because reduced road traffic means less pollution and noise.

e) Good news for business and industry because of improved access to the City, the West End and elsewhere for workers and customers.

f) Good news for tourism and travel generally because of improved access both to Heathrow and the Channel Tunnel.

g) Good news for the construction and engineering industries and the unemployed because it will create work (at least 60,000 person years of employment including between 12,000 and 16,000 jobs at peak; it calls for £450 million worth of rolling stock and £250 million worth of other items).

h) Good news for the disabled because for the first time there will be a railway system actually designed with their needs in mind and based on proper consultation with them.

Potential opponents of Crossrail

Few of these were likely to be a serious threat during the *immediate* danger period because their concerns were not relevant to the government's concern – that is, financing. However, we needed to be aware of them and aware that they would probably attempt some kind of negative response to our campaign.

The main opponents appeared to be:

One or two local councils

The Residents' Association of Mayfair

314 registered objectors – many with individual concerns rather than broader objections

English Heritage

The Church Commissioners

The Theatre Trust

Some MPs.

The main concerns we had to address were:

- The effect of the construction process, including road congestion and other disruption to those living near sites.
- Concern about compensation.
- Noise and vibration from trains.
- The concern of conservationists.
- Suggestions that Crossrail is no longer needed in the wake of decline in rail passengers.

But above all we had to overcome ignorance of Crossrail (which allowed misinformation to flourish) and confusion with other rail projects.

Timing

We had about a month in which to win.

THE CAMPAIGN

Organisation

Policy was determined by a London First Crossrail 'core group' chaired by Peter Foy, senior partner with McKinseys. Management was in the hands of a 'coalition committee' chaired by Stephen O'Brien, London First chief executive. And as director of public affairs for Burson-Marsteller I had responsibility for producing the campaign plan and leading the B-M team which would undertake the bulk of the work.

The 'coalition committee' met weekly for an hour and a wider group of lobbyists employed by the coalition partners also had a weekly meeting. Because of the speed of the campaign, meetings of the key B-M team members took place daily. A Crossrail coalition office was established with its own telephone number and address.

The decision to proceed with a campaign was taken on 19 April and on 23 April I presented the plan to a meeting of the coalition. The first meeting of the coalition committee took place on 26 April.

Media

An early objective was to get the *Evening Standard* further on board (it was already a supporter). Stephen O'Brien and I had a meeting with Stewart Steven, its editor. A promise of further help was secured.

The paper's transport reporter, Dick Murray, was contacted and became the priority recipient of news stories. The *Evening Standard* published two leaders in support of Crossrail, on 6 and 18 May, and major stories on seven days over the next fortnight. There is no question that the newspaper's support was crucial.

Following the media strategy outlined earlier, we otherwise concentrated on the serious national broadsheets, identifying key journalists and appropriate angles for them. At each stage of the campaign press releases were faxed, personally addressed, to target journalists and followed up with telephone calls.

The planned national press conference, attended by an array of top business figures, took place on 6 May and attracted widespread publicity.

On the final weekend before what we knew would be a crucial Cabinet subcommittee meeting, we worked hard to plant stories in the Sunday broadsheets and, from then on, the story developed its own momentum.

Considerable impact was made by a letter sent to *The Times* signed by nine prominent London First leaders. It was perfectly timed, coinciding with the day of the crucial Cabinet subcommittee meeting. BBC Radio 4's 'Today' programme was tipped off about the letter as a peg on which to hang an item.

Lobbying

The committee of lobbyists from other organisations (including representatives of other professional lobbying organisations) met regularly and pooled ideas and resources. It looked at ways of working Crossrail into existing diary engagements of leading supporters and shared mailing lists, and publicised the campaign through newsletters.

Many coalition members had good links with MPs and encouraged their support. I had lunch with a key government minister who was able to give me some useful off-the-record briefing.

Senior members of London First wrote a number of carefully timed letters to the Prime Minister.

The overall effect was to achieve our objective; namely, that the Prime Minister and key Cabinet ministers became aware that support for the project was growing and was influential.

The coalition

We approached a wide variety of interested parties including:

Rail transport
Network South-east
London Regional Transport (LRT)/London Underground Ltd (LUL)
Transport 2000

Commuter organisations (and individuals)
City of London Corporation
London Boroughs Association (LBA)
Association of London Authorities (ALA)
London Planning and Advisory Committee (LPAC)
Buckinghamshire, Berkshire and Essex county councils

District and borough councils
City of Westminster

Commercial property interests
Land Securities
Regalian Properties
Grosvenor Estate Holdings

City, banking, financial and business interests
Confederation of British Industry (CBI)
London Chambers of Commerce and Industry (LCCI)
CENTEC
West London Partnership
East London Partnership
Camden leadership
London Enterprise Agency (LENTA)
Individual companies
Local community and business groups of all kinds

Construction industry
Building Employers Federation
Federation of Civil Engineering Contractors
Manufacturing and Construction Industries Alliance
Taylor Woodrow
John Mowlem
John Laing PLC
Robert McAlpine
Willmott Dixon
Scott Wilson Kilpatrick

Railway engineering industry

The consulting industry
Royal Institute of Chartered Surveyors (RICS)

Road/Motoring organisations
AA
RAC
National Freight Consortium

Tourism and travel interests
British Airports Authority (BAA)
Eurotunnel
London Tourist Board and Convention Bureau
British Airways

Trades unions
including the TGWU
Environmental organisations
Friends of the Earth (FoE)

The disabled
Disabled Living Foundation
Mobility Trust
Joint Committee on Mobility for Disabled People

THE RESULT

The publicity and pressure had the desired effect.

The Prime Minister called together a Cabinet subcommittee to discuss the matter on 18 May. All of our lobbying, media and coalition activity was intensified over the previous weekend and at the beginning of the week of the subcommittee meeting.

The subcommittee took the desired decision and that very evening, at a CBI dinner, the Prime Minister announced that a date for the Crossrail second reading would be fixed. It duly took place a few days later.

The campaign had achieved its objective. To what did it owe its success?

We believe there were five key factors:

- A tight focus on the objective and the 'targets' and a campaign in which all activity was related to them.
- Methodical advance planning.
- Dedication and hard work by team members who worked all hours throughout the campaign.
- Playing to our strengths, including the wide coalition of interests and the influence of key London First figures.
- The involvement of allies and readiness to involve any individual or organisation willing to assist.
- The careful building up of pressure on the right targets with the right arguments.

ACKNOWLEDGEMENTS

My thanks to Hawksmere for their support, and to Leighton Andrews for his contribution. Thanks also to Maurice Frankel, on whose experience of campaign research (particularly as described in our original *Citizen Action* guide) I have drawn heavily.

Special thanks to all the campaigners with whom I've worked who have taught me so much about dedication and professionalism and/or from whom I've had so much support ... not least Eamonn Casey, Cindy Barlow, Eileen Ware and my other colleagues at Shelter; Godfrey Bradman of Citizen Action; Sue Dibb, Robin Russell Jones and Bob Stephens of CLEAR; Jonathan Porritt of FoE; Maurice Frankel, James Cornford and Chris Price of the Campaign for FoI; Henry Witcomb of Citcom; Jane Dunmore, Sam Everington and Anne Leach of PaT; and many who contributed so much to our 1992 general election campaign, including Tim Clement Jones, Peter Lee, Tim Razzell, Gavin Grant, Mark Payne, Simon Titley, Olly Grender, Simon Bryceson, Virginia Morck, Graham Elson, Chris Berry and Elizabeth Jackman. Finally, my thanks, as ever, to my inspirational American friends Ralph Nader and Mike Pertschuk.

NOTES

NOTES

NOTES

NOTES

NOTES

NOTES